THE GREAT
ALLOTMENT
COOKBOOK

THE GREAT
ALLOTMENT
COOKBOOK

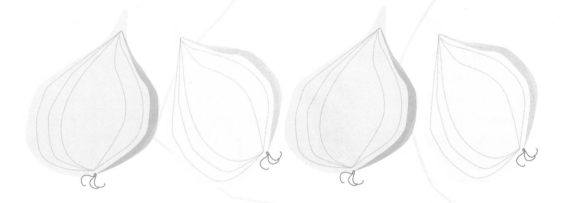

over 200 delicious recipes from plot to plate

An Hachette Livre UK Company
www.hachettelivre.co.uk

First published in Great Britain in
2009 by Gaia, a division of Octopus
Publishing Group Ltd
2-4 Heron Quays, London E14 4JP
www.octopusbooks.co.uk

ISBN 978-1-856-75309-8

A CIP catalogue record for this book
is available from the British Library

Printed and bound in Dubai

10 9 8 7 6 5 4 3 2 1

Notes

Both metric and imperial
measurements have been given in all
recipes. Use one set of measurements
only, and not a mixture of both.

Standard level spoon measurements
are used in all recipes.
1 tablespoon = one 15 ml spoon
1 teaspoon = one 5 ml spoon

The Department of Health advises
that eggs should not be consumed
raw. This book contains dishes made
with raw or lightly cooked eggs. It is
prudent for vulnerable people such as
pregnant and nursing mothers, invalids,
the elderly, babies and young children
to avoid uncooked or lightly cooked
dishes made with eggs. Once
prepared, these dishes should be kept
refrigerated and used promptly.

This book includes dishes made with
nuts and nut derivatives. It is advisable
for customers with known allergic
reactions to nuts and nut derivatives
and those who may be potentially
vulnerable to these allergies, such as
pregnant and nursing mothers, invalids,
the elderly, babies and children, to
avoid dishes made with nuts and
nut oils. It is also prudent to check
the labels of pre-prepared ingredients
for the possible inclusion of
nut derivatives.

Ovens should be preheated to the
specified temperature; if you are
using a fan-assisted oven follow
the manufacturer's instructions
for adjusting the time and
the temperature.

CONTENTS

GROW YOUR OWN

Anyone who has ever had their own allotment, vegetable patch or simply owned a windowbox full of herbs will wax lyrical about the pleasures of growing their own food. It is undoubtedly one of the most rewarding pastimes, and the fruits of your labours will be a continual stock of the most delicious food for you, your family and friends to enjoy.

It takes nothing more than a bit of enthusiasm and energy to get started. Armed with a trowel, some seeds and a watering can you can work the soil, plant your fruit and vegetables and also burn off a few calories at the same time. And soon you will be well on the road to harvesting your very own home-grown produce.

- Your food will be organic.
- You will save money.
- You will never be short of food.
- You will be eating the freshest, most nutritious food available.
- Your crops will be full of flavour, and all the more delicious for the hard work you have invested in them.
- You will keep fit – did you know that 1 hour of digging and hoeing is the equivalent amount of exercise to doing an aerobics class?
- You will reap all the benefits of being outdoors – fresh air, birdsong and the joy of watching your crops grow.
- You will make friends with other growers and can swap seeds, cuttings and expertise.
- You will have a better understanding of the seasons and the food you eat.
- Your diet will be varied and interesting, unlike the bland, shop-bought produce that is available all year round.

HOW TO EAT SEASONALLY

The best way to eat seasonally is to grow your own vegetables and fruit. Because most new houses have relatively small gardens, with little space for a separate vegetable garden, the demand for allotments has been increasing steadily in recent years, and you might find that you have to join a waiting list because of the shortage in your area.

Even if you are not in a position to grow your own food, it doesn't mean that you can't enjoy all the benefits that eating seasonal produce has to offer. These days there are several schemes that will allow you to eat locally grown produce. Why not try one of the following:

- Have an organic fruit and vegetable box delivered to your door.
- Visit a local farm shop or farmers' market.
- Shop at a local greengrocer who sources produce locally.
- Look out for allotments that also have a shop selling excess produce.
- If you have to buy fruit and vegetables in a supermarket, make sure that you know where the produce was grown. Some supermarkets even offer locally grown organic boxes.

There are many benefits to eating locally produced, seasonal fruit. First, your diet will be full of variety, and you won't eat the same old tasteless food day in and day out.

If you eat locally produced vegetables and fruit you will be supporting the local economy and helping producers maintain long-term, viable food production. In addition, you will be reducing energy and CO_2 emissions that are needed to transport food, and your food will be cheaper, because transport costs will be lower. If more people eat locally grown food, demand will be such that suppliers will be able to lower their costs. If you choose organic produce you help will cut down on the use of fertilizers, which are made from oil.

Most important, you will be eating food that is really fresh and packed with nutrients and minerals. Would you rather eat delicious strawberries once a year, or bland tasteless strawberries all year round?

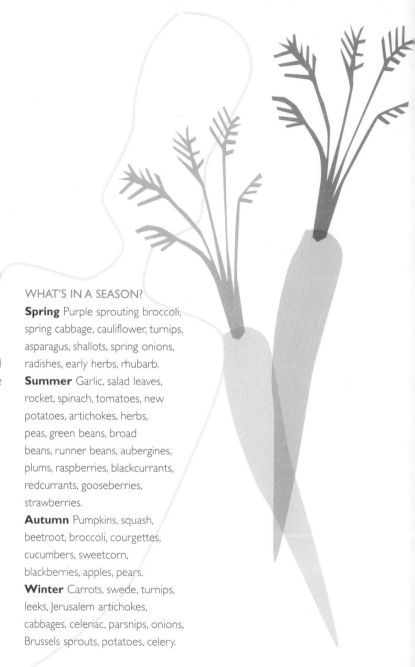

WHAT'S IN A SEASON?

Spring Purple sprouting broccoli, spring cabbage, cauliflower, turnips, asparagus, shallots, spring onions, radishes, early herbs, rhubarb.

Summer Garlic, salad leaves, rocket, spinach, tomatoes, new potatoes, artichokes, herbs, peas, green beans, broad beans, runner beans, aubergines, plums, raspberries, blackcurrants, redcurrants, gooseberries, strawberries.

Autumn Pumpkins, squash, beetroot, broccoli, courgettes, cucumbers, sweetcorn, blackberries, apples, pears.

Winter Carrots, swede, turnips, leeks, Jerusalem artichokes, cabbages, celeriac, parsnips, onions, Brussels sprouts, potatoes, celery.

BEATING THE GLUT

There is nothing worse than food going to waste because you have so much that you don't know what to do with it. With just a little preparation and planning you can stay ahead of the game and utilize everything you harvest. There are so many things you can do with excess fruit and vegetables that there is no need for anything to be wasted.

Preserving, freezing, drying, trading and juicing are all good ways to ensure that you get the best out of your produce, increase its shelf-life and enjoy your food all year round.

FREEZING

Freezing is probably the most obvious way to enjoy your fruit and vegetables throughout the year. If you do it correctly you will also ensure that none of the taste or nutrients is lost in the process. Most vegetables will benefit from being blanched before they are frozen – just a couple of minutes in lightly salted boiling water. Let them go cold, then separate them into portions and put them into freezer bags. Seal them and remember to label them with the contents and date. Most frozen fruit and vegetables will keep for about 6 months.

If you have a lot of berries and would like to use them for preserves add sugar to the fresh berries and pack them tightly into freezer bags so that there is no air in the bag. Once defrosted, the sugar will turn into syrup, which is ideal for jams and jellies. Alternatively, you can simply stew the fruit with sugar and water until it is cooked through. Allow it to go cold and then freeze as above. Stewed fruit is good for pies, cakes and puddings.

Herbs can also be frozen. Chop and freeze them with a little water in ice trays or dry-freeze them in air-free freezer bags. The herbs may discolour slightly but they should still retain their flavour.

PRESERVING

What could be nicer than enjoying homemade strawberry jam on toast or pickled onions with fresh bread and cheese? Preserving your own fruit and vegetables is not only an enjoyable pastime, but it really does make the best of seasonal food all year round. Preserves also make thoughtful gifts that everyone can enjoy. With just a few basic bits of equipment you can get started.

EQUIPMENT
- Large pan
- Sugar thermometer
- Jelly bag
- Spoons
- Funnel
- Clean, dry jars with tops
- Labels
- Wax-coated paper discs

A FEW BASIC RULES

Make sure that all jars are properly washed and sterilized before reusing them. This can be done in your microwave or oven. Add a little water to the jars and put them in a hot oven or microwave for 10 minutes. Alternatively, you can use a dishwasher.

Make sure that the finished preserve is covered with a waxed paper disc before sealing the jar. Put the wax disc face down – waxed side down – on to the hot preserve, secure the lid and leave to cool. As it cools, all the bacteria and spores will be killed. This also applies to chutneys and pickles.

Make sure that each jar is properly labelled with its contents and the date of bottling.

To get the best out of your preserves store them in a cool, dark place and keep them in the refrigerator once they have been opened.

BOTTLING

Bottling fruit in syrup is another way to preserve it, but it can be difficult to get the timing and temperature right. The simplest way is to make sugar syrup using 250 g/8 oz caster sugar and 600 ml/1 pint water. Boil the sugar and water together until the sugar has dissolved. Put the fruit into sterilized jars and pour over the syrup. Stand the jars on a baking sheet in a preheated oven, 150°C/300°F, Gas Mark 2, for up to 40 minutes or until the fruit rises in the syrup.

OTHER WAYS TO PRESERVE

ALCOHOL

Steep the fruit of your choice –
berries, plums and apricots, for
example – in vodka, gin or brandy.
Pierce the small fruits first and cut
larger fruits in halves or quarters
so that they soak up the alcohol.
Add two-thirds alcohol to one-
third sugar and leave to steep
for up to a year. Serve the fruit
with ice cream, in trifles or
in meringues.

VINEGAR

Onions, shallots, ginger, cauliflower
and garlic can all be pickled in
vinegar and bottled.

To make pickled shallots simmer
about 2 litres/3½ pints water, add
250 g/8 oz salt, dissolve the salt
and leave to cool. Add 1.75 kg/3
lb prepared shallots and leave for
24 hours in a cool place. Boil 2
litres/3½ pints malt vinegar with
175 g/6 oz muscovado sugar and
4 tablespoons pickling spices and

allow the mixture to cool. Add
the shallots to the jars, pour over
the vinegar mixture, secure the
lids and leave in a cool dark place
for 3–4 weeks. These quantities
will make 5 jars, each holding
250 g/8 oz.

OIL

A quick and easy way to make a
preserve is to use oil. Onions,
herbs, capers and garlic can all be
preserved this way. Slice your
ingredients and put them in jars,
cover them extra virgin olive oil
and seal. You could also add feta
or goats' cheese. Store the jars at
room temperature.

OVEN-DRYING

Tomatoes, peppers and apples can
be oven-dried, and the dried fruit
and vegetables can be added to
salads, soups and stews. Prepare
your vegetables and place them
on a baking tray, then cook them
in a preheated oven, 120°C/250°F,
Gas Mark ½, for several hours or
until they have dried out and are
crisp. Allow them to cool and
store them in airtight bags or
containers. Oven-dried fruit and
vegetables can be stored for up
to 2–3 weeks.

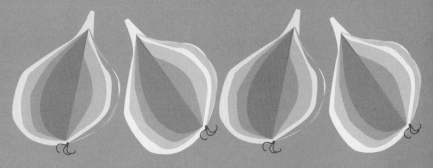

JUICES & SMOOTHIES

Practically all fruit and vegetables make great juices, and if you have a glut of apples or carrots this is one of the best ways of using them. Juices and smoothies are also a great way to make sure your children eat their required portions of fruit and vegetables every day. They are quick and easy to prepare, and homemade juice will surpass anything you can buy.

Smoothies can be made in a food processor or blender, but you will need to invest in a juicer to make the best juice. All you need to do is wash, chop and add your fruit or vegetables to the processor or juicer.

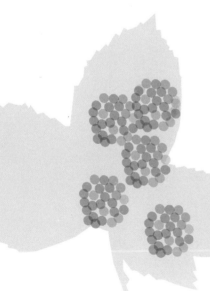

RHUBARB & YOGURT SMOOTHIE

MAKES 200 ML/7 FL OZ

100 g/3^1/$_2$ oz stewed rhubarb

100 g/3^1/$_2$ oz natural yogurt

2 drops of vanilla extract

artificial sweetener, to taste

ice cubes

Put the stewed rhubarb in a blender, add the yogurt, vanilla extract, artificial sweetener and a couple of ice cubes and process until smooth.

Pour the smoothie into a tall glass and serve immediately.

CARROT, APPLE & GINGER JUICE

MAKES 250 ML/8 FL OZ

200 g/7 oz carrots

1 cm/^{1}/$_2$ inch cube fresh root ginger

1 green apple

ice cubes

Scrub the carrots and peel and roughly chop the ginger. Cut the apple and carrots into even-sized pieces and juice them with the ginger.

Pour the juice into a tall glass, add a couple of ice cubes and serve immediately.

BLACKBERRY, APPLE & CELERIAC JUICE

MAKES 200 ML/7 FL OZ

100 g/3½ oz blackberries, plus extra to serve

100 g/3½ oz celeriac

50 g/2 oz apple

ice cubes

🌿 Freeze all the blackberries for at least 2 hours or overnight.

🌿 Peel the celeriac and cut it into chunks. Cut the apple into pieces and juice with the celeriac.

🌿 Transfer the juice to a blender, add the frozen blackberries and a couple of ice cubes and process briefly.

🌿 Pour the juice into a tall glass and serve immediately, decorated with the extra frozen blackberries.

MIXED SUMMER BERRY LASSI

MAKES 300 ML/½ PINT

50 g/2 oz mixed strawberries and raspberries

125 ml/4 fl oz chilled milk

125 ml/4 fl oz chilled natural yogurt

1 teaspoon rosewater

½ teaspoon clear honey

strawberry slices, to serve

🌿 Hull the strawberries. Put all the berries, milk, yogurt and rosewater in a blender and process until smooth.

🌿 Pour the mixture into a tall glass, stir in the honey and serve immediately, decorated with slices of strawberry.

BROCCOLI, BEETROOT & CARROT JUICE

MAKES 200 ML/7 FL OZ

175 g/6 oz carrots

50 g/2 oz beetroot

250 g/8 oz broccoli

sprig of fresh coriander, to serve (optional)

🌿 Scrub the carrots and beetroot. Trim the broccoli. Juice the vegetables.

🌿 Pour the juice into a tall glass and serve garnished with a sprig of coriander, if liked

SHALLOTS ONIONS
SPRING CABBAGE
SPRING GREENS PURPLE
SPROUTING BROCCOLI
SORREL ASPARAGUS
CAULIFLOWER TURNIP
HORSERADISH RHUBARB

FARE

IN SPRING

Lengthening days herald the beginning of spring, and the warmer temperature and increased daylight mean new growth on the allotment. This is a good time to take stock of what's in the freezer and to use up any odds and ends ready for the glut of produce you are likely to have over the coming months. Your dwindling store of root crops will soon make way for fresh spring vegetables such as purple sprouting broccoli, spring cabbage, cauliflower, asparagus and rhubarb. Late spring is perhaps the busiest month in any kitchen garden, when everything is starting to grow, so it is important to stay on top of the weeds before they take over, remember to be vigilant about thinning out seedlings and watch out for the slugs. Most of all enjoy the flavours of spring: try steamed sprouting broccoli, asparagus with Parmesan and rhubarb crumble with cream.

MAKE THE MOST OF...

ASPARAGUS

Asparagus has a short harvest period of about 6–8 weeks. It is important to harvest the asparagus before it develops leaves, but the spears shouldn't be over-cropped because this can affect the success of future crops. Allow the spears to grow until they are 15–20 cm/ 6–8 inches tall. Cut each spear below the soil. The cutting will encourage other buds in the crown to grow. You can store asparagus in the refrigerator for up to a week, standing the spears upright in a small pot of water.

CAULIFLOWER

Cauliflowers are notoriously difficult to grow and leave many gardeners disappointed. If you are successful harvest them while the heads are small and tight. Cut the stem but leave some of the leaves around the head to protect it. Like cabbages (see pages 240–41), they should be eaten as soon as possible, but they can be stored upside down, preferably somewhere cool.

HERBS

Some herbs, including sorrel, chives and chervil, are ready to harvest in spring. Take advantage of these early herbs because they make delicious additions to quiches, sauces and salads. Most herbs if they are cut regularly will come again right through the summer months.

PURPLE SPROUTING BROCCOLI

Pick purple sprouting broccoli when the broccoli has tight purple heads, before the flowers open. If you pick the heads regularly you will encourage sideshoots to develop and have a steady harvest for several months. Once picked, store the florets in the refrigerator for up to 5 days.

RADISHES

Like spring onions, radishes grow quickly, so are ideally suited to succession sowing and are useful for filling gaps in beds when you have lifted other crops. You can also use radish leaves as a spicy addition to salads, and they can be cut and will grow again. Harvest radishes after 4 weeks; pull them up with the help of a hand fork. They will keep for several days in the refrigerator.

RHUBARB

Harvest rhubarb from spring through to summer. Take no more than half of the stems at any one time. Pull each stem at the base and twist – it should come away easily. Rhubarb keeps well in the refrigerator for several weeks; it can also be frozen and cooked from raw.

SHALLOTS

Shallots, which grow in bulb clusters, are among the easiest crops to grow. Wait until the leaves start to turn yellow before you harvest them. Use a hand fork to ease the bulbs carefully from the soil, separate them and allow them to dry out for a day. They can be hung in a cool, dry place and will be usable for months.

SPRING CABBAGE

Spring cabbages tend to be smaller and more pointed than their later cousins. To harvest them make sure you cut them as close to the ground as possible; alternatively you can just pull off leaves as and when you require them. If you score the leftover stump with a cross the plant should produce more heads in 4–6 weeks. Cabbages should be eaten as quickly as possible after harvesting because they don't store well.

SPRING ONIONS

Use a hand fork to lift spring onions out of the ground when the bulbs are about 2.5 cm/1 inch in diameter. Continue to sow the seeds at 3-week intervals from mid-spring to early summer for a succession of crops throughout the season.

TURNIPS

The first turnips appear in mid-spring; they can be pulled from the ground when they are about the size of a table tennis ball. If they are left to grow too big they will lack flavour and become woody in texture. If you can't eat them straightaway store them in a cool, dry place.

CAMEMBERT & SHALLOT TARTS

TAKES 30 MINS
FEEDS 4

50 g/2 oz butter

8 large shallots, each cut into 4 wedges

1 tablespoon chopped lemon thyme

350 g/11½ oz puff pastry, thawed if frozen

125 g/4 oz Camembert cheese, sliced

salt and pepper

Lightly grease a baking sheet and sprinkle it with water. Melt the butter in a frying pan, add the shallots and fry gently for 5 minutes until softened. Stir in the thyme.

Roll out the pastry on a lightly floured surface to a 20 cm/8 inch square and cut it into 4 squares. Transfer these to the prepared baking sheet. Use the tip of a sharp knife to make a shallow cut along each side of the squares, 1 cm/½ inch in from the edges, to form a rim.

Spoon the shallots and thyme into the centres of the pastries. Bake in a preheated oven, 220°C/425°F/Gas Mark 7, for 10 minutes until well risen. Arrange the cheese over the shallots and return to the oven for a further 5 minutes. Serve warm.

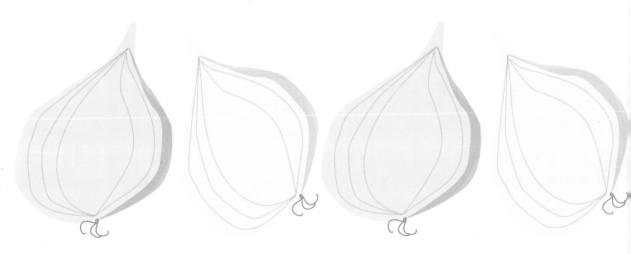

PASTRY

175 g/6 oz self-raising
wholemeal flour

75 g/3 oz chilled butter, diced

2 tablespoons chopped parsley

2 teaspoons chopped thyme

2–3 tablespoons lemon juice

TOPPING

500 g/1 lb shallots, peeled

25 g/1 oz butter

2 tablespoons olive oil

2 teaspoons muscovado sugar

salt and pepper

🌿 Make the pastry. Put the flour in a bowl. Add the butter and rub in with your fingertips until the mixture resembles fine breadcrumbs. Stir in the parsley, thyme and lemon juice and mix to a firm dough. Knead briefly.

🌿 Make the topping. Boil the shallots in a pan of water for 10 minutes, then drain well. Heat the butter and oil in an ovenproof frying pan, add the shallots and fry gently, stirring, for about 10 minutes, until they are starting to colour. Sprinkle over the sugar, season to taste and cook gently for a further 5 minutes, until the shallots are well coloured. Remove the pan from the heat.

🌿 Roll out the dough on a lightly floured surface to a round, a little larger than the pan. Support the dough over the rolling pin and place it over the shallots, tucking the edges of the pastry down the side of the pan. Bake the tart in a preheated oven, 200°C/400°F/Gas Mark 6, for 20–25 minutes, until the pastry is crisp.

🌿 Leave the tart in the pan for 5 minutes to cool, then place a large plate over the pan and invert the tart on to it. Serve warm or cold.

ONION TART TATIN

To make the onions easier to peel, plunge them into boiling water for 30 seconds, then drain. When they are cool enough to handle, peel off the skins, but avoid trimming the root ends, or the onions will lose their shape during cooking.

Heat the oil in a large, heavy-based frying pan over a medium heat. Stir in the onions, arranging them in a single layer, then add enough water so that the onions are half immersed in liquid. Bring to a gentle simmer and cook for 30 minutes, stirring occasionally. If most of the liquid evaporates, add a couple of tablespoons of hot water.

Stir in the balsamic vinegar and sugar and season to taste with salt and pepper. Stir well to combine and continue to cook, stirring occasionally, for a further 1½ hours, adding more water when the pan dries out, until the onions are soft all the way through and caramelized to a golden colour with a rich glaze. Serve at room temperature as part of an antipasto selection.

TAKES 2 ¼ HRS
SERVES 4–6 AS AN ANTIPASTO

625 g/1¼ lb baby onions
1 tablespoon olive oil
2 tablespoons balsamic vinegar
½ teaspoon caster sugar
salt and pepper

SWEET AND SOUR BABY ONIONS

FOOD FOR

SPRING CABBAGE WITH PANCETTA

TAKES 15 MINS
SERVES 4

1 tablespoon olive oil

1 onion, sliced

1 garlic clove, crushed

1 red chilli, cored, deseeded and diced

125 g/4 oz pancetta, diced

1 head of spring cabbage

75 ml/3 fl oz chicken stock

75 g/3 oz Parmesan cheese, coarsely grated

salt and pepper

Heat the oil in a large saucepan, add the onion, garlic, chilli and pancetta and sauté for 5 minutes or until soft.

Trim any wilting leaves from the cabbage and cut the head in half lengthways. Remove and discard the hard central stem and roughly chop the leaves.

Add the cabbage to the onion mixture and stir well. Pour in the stock and season to taste with salt and pepper. Cook for 4 minutes over a moderate heat, stirring constantly.

Add the grated Parmesan and serve immediately.

THE PICKING

BLACK BEAN & CABBAGE STEW

4 tablespoons olive oil

1 large onion, chopped

1 leek, chopped

3 garlic cloves, sliced

1 tablespoon paprika

2 tablespoons chopped marjoram or thyme

625 g/1 1/4 lb potatoes, cut into small chunks

425 g/14 oz can black beans or black-eyed beans, rinsed and drained

1 litre/1 3/4 pints vegetable stock

175 g/6 oz cabbage or spring greens, shredded

salt and pepper

crusty bread, to serve

Heat the oil in a large saucepan. Add the onion and leek and fry gently for 3 minutes. Add the garlic and paprika and fry for 2 minutes.

Add the marjoram or thyme, potatoes, beans and stock and bring to the boil. Reduce the heat, cover and simmer gently for about 10 minutes until the potatoes have softened but are not mushy.

Add the cabbage or spring greens and season to taste with salt and pepper. Serve immediately with crusty bread.

Put the brown rice in a large saucepan of boiling water with the seaweed and bring to the boil. Reduce the heat a little and cook at a fast simmer for 30 minutes. When the rice is just cooked and still retains a bite, drain well (reserving some of the cooking water) and discard the seaweed.

Meanwhile, heat the oil in a large frying pan or wok and gently cook the onion until golden-brown and crisp. Add the garlic and continue to cook gently for 1 minute, stirring constantly, to flavour the oil. Do not allow the garlic to burn.

Add the spring greens and ginger and stir-fry for 1–2 minutes or until the greens are just wilted.

Combine the tamari or soy sauce, sesame oil and 6 tablespoons of the reserved rice cooking water. Add the liquid to the vegetables and stir-fry for 1 minute.

Remove from the heat and toss together the cooked rice and the wilted spring greens. Spoon into serving bowls and top with toasted sesame seeds and pepper. Serve immediately or chill and serve cold.

**TAKES 45 MINS
SERVES 4**

250 g/8 oz brown rice

10 cm/4 inches dried kombu seaweed

3 tablespoons olive oil

1 onion, finely chopped

2 garlic cloves, crushed

325 g/11 oz spring greens, shredded

8 cm/3 inches fresh root ginger, finely chopped

4 tablespoons tamari or soy sauce

1 tablespoon sesame oil

2 tablespoons sesame seeds, toasted

pepper

WILTED SPRING GREENS WITH GINGER

Carefully pick over the cabbage leaves, discarding any that are blemished. Shred the cabbage.

Combine the vinaigrette dressing with the soy sauce. Put the spring cabbage into a bowl with the dressing, mix thoroughly and leave to marinate for I hour.

Add the celery, spring onions and red pepper to the spring cabbage and mix thoroughly. Serve, garnished with pepper strips.

SPRING CABBAGE & PEPPER SALAD

TAKES 15 MINS, PLUS MARINATING
SERVES 6

250 g/8 oz spring cabbage

50 ml/2 fl oz light vinaigrette dressing

I teaspoon light soy sauce

3 celery sticks, sliced

4 spring onions, chopped

I red pepper, cored, deseeded and diced

red pepper strips, to garnish

PURPLE SPROUTING BROCCOLI WITH AVGOLEMONO SAUCE

TAKES 20–22 MINS
SERVES 6

400 g/13 oz purple sprouting broccoli

4 egg yolks

4 tablespoons lemon juice

200 ml/7 fl oz hot chicken or vegetable stock

salt and pepper

🌿 Arrange the broccoli in a single layer in the top of a steamer, cover and cook for 10–12 minutes until just tender.

🌿 Meanwhile, put the egg yolks and a little salt and pepper into a bowl set above simmering water. Use a handheld electric or balloon whisk to beat the yolks, then whisk in the lemon juice, a little at a time.

🌿 Gradually whisk in the hot stock and continue whisking until the sauce is thick and frothy. This should take 7–10 minutes in all.

🌿 Transfer the broccoli to a warm serving dish. Serve the sauce separately in a warm jug.

ANCHOVY & PURPLE SPROUTING BROCCOLI BRUSCHETTA

TAKES 20 MINS
SERVES 4

4 tablespoons olive oil

pinch of dried red chilli flakes

pared rind of 1 lemon

2 garlic cloves, crushed

4 anchovy fillets in oil, drained and chopped

625 g/1¼ lb purple sprouting broccoli, cut into pieces

1 tablespoon lemon juice

4 slices of sourdough bread

pepper

Parmesan shavings, to garnish

Heat the oil in a small saucepan and gently fry the chilli, lemon rind, garlic and anchovy fillets for 1–2 minutes until softened but not browned. The anchovy should start to melt into the oil. Remove the pan from the heat and keep warm.

Cook the broccoli in a saucepan of lightly salted boiling water for 3 minutes until just tender. Drain thoroughly and return to the pan. Add the anchovy mixture, lemon juice and some pepper and toss until the broccoli is evenly coated.

Meanwhile, toast the bread on both sides. Arrange it on plates and top with the broccoli mixture. Serve garnished with Parmesan shavings.

TIME 35 MINS
SERVES 4

50 g/2 oz walnuts, roughly chopped

4 halibut fillets, each about 175 g/6 oz, skinned

25 g/1 oz butter

2 tablespoons walnut oil

1 shallot, finely chopped

50 g/2 oz pancetta, chopped

200 g/7 oz sorrel, tough stalks removed

100 ml/3½ fl oz crème fraîche

salt and pepper

Lightly toast the walnuts in a large frying pan and tip them on to a plate. Lightly season the halibut.

Melt the butter with the oil in a heavy-based frying pan and gently fry the shallot and pancetta for about 5 minutes or until golden. Remove with a slotted spoon.

Add the halibut fillets to the pan and fry for 2–3 minutes on each side until cooked through. Remove the halibut and keep warm. Add the sorrel to the pan and cook briefly until the leaves wilt. Tip the sorrel on to warm serving plates and top with the fish.

Return the shallot and pancetta to the pan and add the crème fraîche. Heat through, season to taste with salt and pepper and spoon over the fish. Serve immediately.

HALIBUT WITH SORREL & PANCETTA

ASPARAGUS

PATIENCE PLAYS DIVIDENDS WHEN YOU ARE GROWING ASPARAGUS. IT CAN TAKE UP TO 3 YEARS FOR THE FIRST SPEARS TO APPEAR, BUT ONCE THE PLANTS ARE ESTABLISHED THEY ARE HERE TO STAY AND CAN PRODUCE A GOOD CROP FOR 20 YEARS. ALTHOUGH THE SEASON IS SHORT, ABOUT 8 WEEKS, YOU WILL NOT BE DISAPPOINTED BECAUSE ASPARAGUS IS BOTH DELICIOUS AND VERSATILE.

ASPARAGUS BELONGS TO THE LILY FAMILY AND IS NATIVE TO MEDITERRANEAN COUNTRIES. IT CAN BE TRACED BACK TO THE 1ST CENTURY AD, BUT IT HAS BECOME A FAVOURITE IN NORTHERN EUROPE AND NORTH AMERICA ONLY SINCE THE 16TH CENTURY. QUICK AND EASY TO COOK, IT IS NO LONGER SEEN AS A VEGETABLE FOR THE RICH AND FAMOUS BUT AS SOMETHING THAT IS ACCESSIBLE TO EVERYONE.

GOOD FOR YOU

Asparagus is good for the skin, hair and nails because it is rich in vitamins C and E, and it is one of the few vegetables that contains folic acid, which is all important for expectant mothers. The spears are high in fibre and rich in potassium, so this vegetable is a great protector against many serious diseases and is good for boosting the immune system. Historically, it was also thought to be an aphrodisiac, so it could be good for your love life too.

FIVE OF THE BEST

Connover's Colossal A high-yielding asparagus with bright green spears and purple tips. It freezes well.

Martha Washington A strong-growing, rust-resistant cultivar, with thick spears that are tasty and meaty.

Jersey Knight The delicious spears are thick, yet tender.

Cito A popular and reliable asparagus that will cope with most conditions.

Gijnlim A cultivar that has been known to crop after just one year, it is consistent and has mid-green spears with purple tips.

DELICIOUS IDEAS TO TRY

Roast Roast for 20 minutes in a hot oven with a dash of olive oil and a sprinkling of salt. Serve with white fish or chicken.

Steam Steam your asparagus until just tender, about 5 minutes, then serve as dippers with runny boiled eggs.

Wrap Wrap the spears in pancetta and roast for 15–20 minutes in a medium-hot oven. This dish makes a great starter or party nibble.

Sauce Whisk 3 egg yolks in a saucepan with a tablespoon of lemon juice, a pinch of cayenne pepper and salt and pepper to taste. Dice 250 g/8 oz butter and add to the pan, whisking continuously over medium heat until thickened. Serve this hollandaise sauce with steamed asparagus.

Salad Mix some hot cooked new potatoes with steamed asparagus and chopped red onion. Drizzle with a dressing of Dijon mustard, white wine vinegar and olive oil. Top with chopped flat leaf parsley.

TOP TIPS FOR ASPARAGUS

To store asparagus, stand the spears in a pot of water and refrigerate.

Asparagus spears have an outer membrane that needs to be removed with a vegetable peeler before cooking.

Eat asparagus while it's really fresh because it deteriorates very rapidly.

Trim the ends of the asparagus and cut the spears into 2.5 cm/1 inch segments. Bring the measured water, lightly salted, to the boil, add the asparagus and cook for 15 minutes or until very tender. Drain, reserving the liquid in a jug.

Melt the butter in a large, heavy-based saucepan, stir in the flour and cook over a moderate heat, stirring constantly, for 1 minute. Gradually add the reserved liquid. Bring to the boil, stirring constantly, and cook until thickened. Add the nutmeg and salt and pepper to taste and cook, stirring frequently, for 3–5 minutes.

Add the asparagus and reduce the heat. Simmer gently, stirring occasionally, for 5 minutes.

Beat the egg yolks in a small bowl with the cream and add a little pepper. Pour into the soup, stir well and cook for 1 minute without boiling. Serve the soup in warm bowls, garnishing each portion with a sprinkling of snipped chives.

TAKES 40 MINS
SERVES 6

1 kg/2 lb asparagus
2 litres/3$^{1}/_{2}$ pints water
25 g/1 oz butter
1 tablespoon plain flour
pinch of grated nutmeg
2 egg yolks
300 ml/$^{1}/_{2}$ pint double cream
salt and white pepper
1 tablespoon snipped chives, to garnish

CREAM OF ASPARAGUS SOUP

SCALLOPS WITH GINGER & ASPARAGUS

TAKES 20 MINS, PLUS MARINATING
SERVES 4

12 fresh scallops

2 spring onions, thinly sliced

finely grated rind of I lime

I tablespoon ginger cordial

**2 tablespoons olive oil, plus
extra to drizzle**

**250 g/8 oz thin asparagus
spears**

juice of ¹/₂ lime

mixed salad leaves

sprigs of chervil, to garnish

salt and pepper

Discard the coral and the tough muscle from the side of each scallop. Wash the scallops and pat them dry, then cut each one in half and place them in a bowl.

Mix together the spring onions, lime rind, ginger cordial and half the oil and season to taste with salt and pepper. Pour this dressing over the scallops and set aside to marinate for 15 minutes.

Meanwhile, steam the asparagus spears in lightly salted boiling water for 5–8 minutes until tender. Lift out with a slotted spoon and toss them with the remaining oil and the lime juice. Season to taste with salt and pepper and keep warm.

Heat a large, nonstick frying pan. Drain the scallops (reserving the marinade) and fry for 1 minute on each side until golden and just cooked through. Stir in the marinade juices.

Arrange the asparagus spears, salad leaves and chervil on plates with the scallops, pour over the pan juices and serve.

Arrange the asparagus in a single layer in a shallow dish. Drizzle over the oil and season to taste with salt and pepper. Gently turn the asparagus to coat evenly with the oil.

Meanwhile, make the lemon mayonnaise. Beat together all the ingredients in a small bowl and season to taste with salt and pepper. Cover and set aside.

Heat a large, heavy-based griddle pan over a high heat until smoking. Add the asparagus, in batches, and cook for 2–3 minutes on each side or until lightly charred at the edges. Remove from the pan and keep hot while you cook the remaining asparagus. Serve hot with the lemon mayonnaise.

TAKES 15 MINS
SERVES 4

800 g/1 lb 10 oz asparagus spears, trimmed and bases peeled

3 tablespoons olive oil

salt and pepper

LEMON MAYONNAISE

200 ml/7 fl oz mayonnaise

2 garlic cloves, crushed

2 teaspoons finely grated lemon rind

2 tablespoons lemon juice

pinch of pimentón dulce (mild paprika)

GRIDDLED ASPARAGUS WITH LEMON MAYONNAISE

BALSAMIC-GLAZED SWORDFISH WITH ASPARAGUS

TAKES 33 MINS, PLUS MARINATING
SERVES 4

100 ml/3¹/₂ fl oz aged reduced
balsamic vinegar

5 tablespoons olive oil

1 tablespoon harissa

2 tablespoons green olive
paste

4 thick swordfish steaks, each
about 200 g/7 oz

75 g/3 oz small black Tuscan
olives, pitted

300 g/10 oz asparagus spears

salt and pepper

Mix together the balsamic vinegar, 3 tablespoons of the oil, the harissa and green olive paste in a large bowl. Add the swordfish steaks and leave to marinate for about 1 hour.

Remove the fish from the marinade, pat dry with kitchen paper and set aside. Pour the marinade into a small saucepan and heat gently until bubbling. Leave to simmer for 2–3 minutes, then remove from the heat.

Put the olives and remaining olive oil in a bowl, add the asparagus spears and toss well. Season generously with salt and pepper and tip into a roasting tin. Bake in a preheated oven, 190°C/375°F/Gas Mark 5, for about 12 minutes until the asparagus is cooked and golden.

Heat a nonstick frying pan and cook the swordfish steaks for 6–8 minutes, turning them once, until they are almost cooked through.

Arrange the asparagus spears and olives on warm serving plates, top with the swordfish steaks and drizzle over the balsamic glaze. Serve immediately.

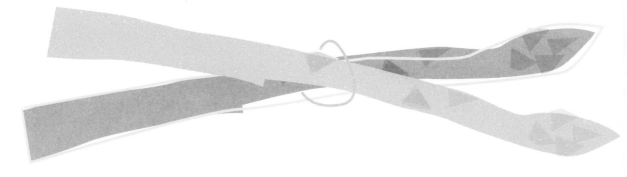

Cook the pasta in a large saucepan of boiling water for 10–12 minutes or according to the instructions on the packet until it is just tender. Drain and return to the pan.

Meanwhile, cook the asparagus tips in a saucepan of boiling water for 2 minutes or until just tender. Drain.

Mix the smoked salmon, fromage frais, asparagus, tarragon and a little grated nutmeg into the pasta and serve immediately.

**TAKES 15–17 MINS
SERVES 2**

**125–175 g/4–6 oz dried
wholewheat spaghetti**

150 g/5 oz asparagus tips

**125 g/4 oz smoked
salmon, cut into pieces**

**4 heaped tablespoons
fromage frais**

**2 tablespoons chopped
tarragon**

grated nutmeg

SMOKED SALMON & ASPARAGUS WHOLEWHEAT SPAGHETTI

DIG FOR YO

SPAGHETTI WITH ROASTED ASPARAGUS & ANCHOVIES

TAKES 25–27 MINS
SERVES 4

375 g/12 oz dried spaghetti

375 g/12 oz asparagus, trimmed and cut into 8 cm/3 inch lengths

5 tablespoons olive oil

50 g/2 oz butter

$^{1}/_{2}$ teaspoon crushed dried chilli flakes

2 garlic cloves, sliced

50 g/2 oz anchovy fillets in oil, drained and chopped

2 tablespoons lemon juice

75 g/3 oz Parmesan cheese shavings

salt

Cook the pasta in a large saucepan of lightly salted boiling water for 10–12 minutes or according to the instructions on the packet until it is just tender. Drain well.

Meanwhile, put the asparagus in a roasting tin, drizzle with olive oil and dot with the butter. Scatter over the chilli, garlic and anchovies and cook in a preheated oven, 200°C/400°F/Gas Mark 6, for 8 minutes until tender.

Toss the asparagus with the hot pasta and squeeze over the lemon juice. Scatter the Parmesan over the top, season with salt and serve immediately.

BAKED ASPARAGUS FRITTATA

TAKES 37–40 MINS
SERVES 4

250 g/8 oz asparagus, trimmed and halved

1 tablespoon olive oil

2 leeks, trimmed and sliced

2 garlic cloves, crushed

2 tablespoons chopped basil

6 eggs

2 tablespoons milk

2 tablespoons grated Parmesan cheese

salt and pepper

Cook the asparagus in a saucepan of lightly salted boiling water for 2 minutes, then drain and shake dry.

Meanwhile, heat the oil in a frying pan and gently fry the leeks and garlic for 5 minutes until they are soft. Add the asparagus and basil and remove the pan from the heat.

Beat together the eggs and the milk and season to taste with salt and pepper. Stir in the vegetable mixture and pour into a greased 1.2 litre/2 pint ovenproof dish. Scatter over the Parmesan and cook in a preheated oven, 200°C/400°F/Gas Mark 6, for 15–20 minutes until the frittata is firm in the centre. Serve warm, cut into pieces.

GOOD EATING

5 tablespoons passata (puréed tomatoes)

1 tablespoon red pesto

4 x 25 cm/10 inch ready-made pizza bases

250 g/8 oz taleggio cheese, derinded and sliced

175 g/6 oz thin asparagus spears, trimmed

2 tablespoons olive oil

salt and pepper

Mix together the passata and pesto, add a pinch of salt and spread the mixture over the pizza bases. Top with the Taleggio and asparagus and drizzle with olive oil.

Place the pizzas directly on the shelves of a preheated oven, 200°C/400°F/Gas Mark 6, and cook for 10 minutes until the asparagus is tender and the pizza bases crisp. Grind over some fresh black pepper before serving.

ASPARAGUS & TALEGGIO PIZZA

Make the dressing. Mix together the vinegar, garlic, tomatoes and olive oil in a bowl. Set aside.

Brush the asparagus with the oil and cook on an oiled barbecue grill over moderately hot coals for 5–6 minutes until tender. Alternatively, cook under a preheated hot grill for 4–5 minutes, turning frequently until tender.

Transfer the grilled asparagus to 4 warm serving plates. Spoon over the balsamic and tomato dressing, top with pine nuts and Parmesan slivers and sprinkle with the sea salt and pepper. Serve immediately.

TAKES 15 MINS
SERVES 4

500 g/1 lb young asparagus spears, trimmed

2 tablespoons olive oil

50 g/2 oz pine nuts, toasted

25 g/1 oz Parmesan cheese, shaved into thin slivers

sea salt flakes and pepper

BALSAMIC AND TOMATO DRESSING

2 tablespoons balsamic vinegar

1–2 garlic cloves, crushed

375 g/12 oz tomatoes, skinned, deseeded and chopped

5 tablespoons olive oil

ASPARAGUS WITH BALSAMIC & TOMATO DRESSING

GRILLED ASPARAGUS WITH WALNUT SAUCE

TAKES 12–14 MINS
SERVES 4

1 kg/2 lb asparagus spears, trimmed

25 g/1 oz Parmesan cheese, grated (optional)

salt and pepper

WALNUT SAUCE

50 g/2 oz walnuts, toasted

2 large spring onions, finely chopped

1 garlic clove, crushed

1 teaspoon grated lemon rind

1 tablespoon chopped basil

1 tablespoon chopped parsley

4 tablespoons walnut oil, plus extra for brushing

50 ml/2 fl oz milk

Make the sauce. Whizz the walnuts with the spring onions, garlic, lemon rind and herbs. Whisk in the oil and then the milk to form a fairly smooth pouring sauce.

Brush the asparagus spears with oil and cook under a preheated hot grill for 5–6 minutes, turning frequently until golden and tender.

Transfer the asparagus to a warm gratin dish, pour over the sauce and sprinkle over the cheese (if used). Return to the grill for 1–2 minutes until bubbling and golden. Serve immediately.

Bring a large saucepan of lightly salted water to the boil. Break the cauliflower florets into bite-sized pieces, add them to the pan and cook for 6–8 minutes. Drain thoroughly and set aside.

Heat the oil in a large, nonstick frying pan. Add the garlic and cook over a medium heat, stirring, for 1–2 minutes. Add the cauliflower, pimentón and vinegar and season to taste with salt and pepper. Cook over a high heat, stirring, for 3–4 minutes, then remove from the heat.

Sprinkle the cauliflower with some chopped flat leaf parsley to garnish and serve immediately.

SPANISH GARLIC CAULIFLOWER

TAKES 10–14 MINS
SERVES 4

800 g/1 lb 10 oz cauliflower florets

4 tablespoons olive oil

3 garlic cloves, finely chopped

1 tablespoon pimentón dulce (mild paprika)

2 tablespoons white wine vinegar

salt and pepper

finely chopped flat leaf parsley, to garnish

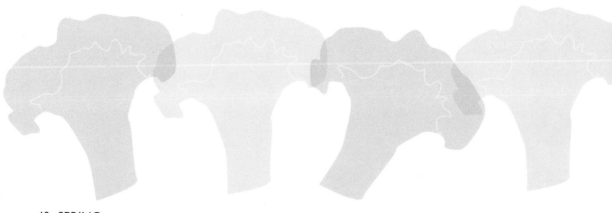

TAKES 30 MINS
SERVES 6–8

2 teaspoons olive oil

2 garlic cloves, finely chopped

1–2 small red chillies, sliced lengthways and deseeded

1/2 small cauliflower, cut into small florets

125 ml/4 fl oz chicken stock

125 ml/4 fl oz dry white wine

500 g/1 lb fresh ribbed penne

50 g/2 oz small pitted black olives

salt

PENNE WITH CHILLI & CAULIFLOWER

Heat the oil in a large, heavy-based pan. Add the garlic and cook until soft and golden. Add the chillies and cook for about 30 seconds, then remove the garlic and chillies from the pan with a slotted spoon and set aside.

Add the cauliflower florets, stock and wine to the pan. Cover and cook for 6–8 minutes or until the cauliflower is just tender. Remove the cauliflower from the pan and keep it warm.

Rinse the pan, fill it with lightly salted water and bring to the boil. Add the pasta and cook according to the instructions on the packet or until it is just tender. Drain well.

Put the pasta into a warm serving bowl. Add the cauliflower florets, garlic, chillies and olives. Toss to combine and serve immediately.

Heat a heavy-based frying pan and melt the butter. Add the breadcrumbs and hazelnuts and stir-fry over a medium heat for about 3 minutes until crisp and golden. Drain on kitchen paper and set aside.

Bring a large pan of water to the boil, add 1 teaspoon salt and the pasta. Return to the boil and cook over a medium heat for 10–12 minutes until the pasta is just tender.

Meanwhile, heat half the oil in a pan and fry the cauliflower, garlic and chilli for 8–10 minutes until the cauliflower is golden and tender. Add the parsley.

Drain the pasta, toss it with the remaining oil and some pepper and stir into the cauliflower mixture. Serve immediately, topped with the crispy breadcrumb mixture.

CAULIFLOWER WITH BREADCRUMBS & HAZELNUTS

TAKES 20–25 MINS
SERVES 4

25 g/1 oz butter

50 g/2 oz fresh white breadcrumbs

25 g/1 oz hazelnuts, finely chopped

375 g/12 oz dried fusilli

8 tablespoons hazelnut oil

1 cauliflower, divided into tiny florets

2 garlic cloves, sliced

1 dried red chilli, deseeded and chopped

2 tablespoons chopped parsley

salt and pepper

PLOT TO

PAN-FRIED FILLET STEAK & ROQUEFORT SAUCE

TAKES 14–15 MINS
SERVES 4

25 g/1 oz butter

4 fillet steaks, each about 150 g/5 oz

cauliflower mash, to serve

ROQUEFORT SAUCE

1 garlic clove, crushed

25 g/1 oz parsley, roughly chopped

15 g/¹/₂ oz mint, roughly chopped

1 tablespoon roughly chopped walnuts

75 ml/3 fl oz olive oil

2 tablespoons walnut oil

50 g/2 oz Roquefort cheese, crumbled

15 g/¹/₂ oz Parmesan cheese, grated

salt and pepper

 Make the sauce. Put the garlic, parsley, mint, walnuts and oils in a food processor and whizz until fairly smooth. Add both cheeses, whizz again and season to taste with salt and pepper.

 Heat the butter in a heavy-based frying pan. Season the steaks to taste with salt and pepper, add them to the pan and cook for 2 minutes each side for rare or a little longer for medium rare.

 Transfer the steaks to warm serving plates, top with the cheese sauce and serve immediately with cauliflower mash.

PLATE

BUTTERED CAULIFLOWER CRUMBLE

TIME 20 MINS
SERVES 4

I large cauliflower

25 g/1 oz butter

50 g/2 oz breadcrumbs

2 tablespoons olive oil

3 tablespoons capers

3 cocktail gherkins, finely chopped

3 tablespoons chopped dill or tarragon

100 ml/3½ fl oz crème fraîche

4 tablespoons grated Parmesan cheese

salt and pepper

Cut the cauliflower into large florets and blanch in boiling water for 2 minutes. Drain thoroughly.

Melt half the butter in a large, heavy-based frying pan. Add the breadcrumbs and fry for 2 minutes until golden. Drain and set aside.

Melt the remaining butter in the pan with the oil. Add the cauliflower florets and fry gently for about 5 minutes until golden. Add the capers, gherkins, dill or tarragon and crème fraîche, season to taste with salt and pepper and stir over a moderate heat for 1 minute.

Turn the cauliflower mixture into a shallow flameproof dish and sprinkle with the fried breadcrumbs and Parmesan. Cook under a preheated moderate grill for about 2 minutes until the crumbs are dark golden brown. Serve immediately.

Heat the oil in a large, nonstick frying pan. Add the mustard seeds, turmeric and asafoetida. When the seeds start to pop, add the cauliflower, onion and chilli. Stir-fry for 5 minutes, then remove from the heat. The cauliflower should have bite to it.

Season the relish with lemon juice and salt to taste. Serve at room temperature.

CAULIFLOWER RELISH

TAKES 17–18 MINS
MAKES ABOUT 400 G/13 OZ

2 tablespoons vegetable oil

2 teaspoons black mustard seeds

$1/2$ teaspoon ground turmeric

$1/2$ teaspoon asafoetida

I small cauliflower, cut into bite-sized pieces

I red onion, finely chopped

I fresh green chilli, halved, deseeded and finely chopped

lemon juice

sea salt

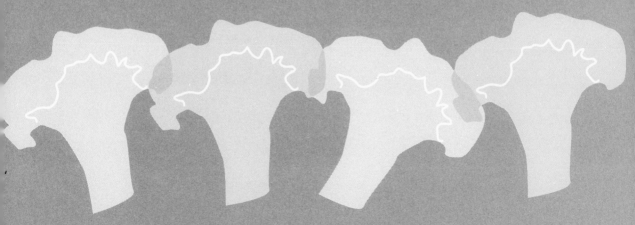

Heat the oil in a large frying pan. Add the baby onions or shallots and garlic, cover and cook over a low heat, stirring occasionally, for 10–12 minutes until the onions or shallots are soft. Add the potatoes and cook over a medium-low heat, stirring frequently, for 3–4 minutes. Remove from the heat, cover and keep warm.

Bring a saucepan of lightly salted water to the boil, add the carrots and cook for 6–8 minutes or until just tender. Add the broad beans and cook for 2–3 minutes. Drain and transfer to the onion or shallot and potato mixture.

Add the crème fraîche, season to taste with salt and pepper and toss to combine. Return the stew to the heat and cook over a high heat, stirring, for 2–3 minutes. Serve immediately, garnished with sliced spring onions.

**TAKES 23–30 MINS
SERVES 4**

2 tablespoons olive oil

100 g/3^1/$_2$ oz baby onions or small shallots, peeled but left whole

2 garlic cloves, finely chopped

250 g/8 oz baby new potatoes, peeled and cooked until just tender

250 g/8 oz baby carrots, trimmed and halved or quartered if large

250 g/8 oz shelled broad beans, fresh or frozen

2 tablespoons crème fraîche

salt and pepper

spring onions, sliced, to garnish

SPRING VEGETABLE STEW

BACON & TURNIP SOUP

TAKES 1 HR
SERVES 6

25 g/1 oz butter

125 g/4 oz rindless smoked
bacon, roughly chopped

1 onion, roughly chopped

375 g/12 oz potatoes, chopped

750 g/1 ½ lb turnips, chopped

1.2 litres/2 pints chicken stock

1 bay leaf

small sprig of thyme

150 ml/¼ pint milk

salt and pepper

finely chopped parsley, to garnish

Melt the butter in a large, heavy-based saucepan. Add the bacon and cook over a moderate heat until crisp and golden. Remove with a slotted spoon and reserve.

Add the onion, potatoes and turnips to the bacon fat and cook over a low heat for about 5 minutes. Add the stock, bay leaf and thyme and bring to the boil, then reduce the heat and cook for 30–35 minutes or until all the vegetables are tender. Remove and discard the bay leaf and thyme sprig.

Put the soup in a food processor or blender and whizz, in batches if necessary, until smooth. Transfer to a clean saucepan, add the reserved bacon and the milk and reheat gently without boiling. Serve immediately in warm soup bowls, sprinkled with a little parsley.

TAKES 18–20 MINS
SERVES 4–6

500 g/1 lb baby turnips

1 red onion, thinly sliced

handful of flat leaf parsley,
roughly torn

coarse sea salt and pepper

SWEET MUSTARD DRESSING

3 tablespoons olive oil

2 tablespoons wholegrain
mustard

1 tablespoon clear honey

1 teaspoon white wine vinegar or
lemon juice

salt and pepper

Cook the baby turnips in a pan of boiling water for 8–10 minutes; they should still be slightly crisp. Drain and refresh under cold running water, then drain thoroughly.

Make the dressing. Put the oil, mustard, honey and vinegar or lemon juice in a small bowl, season to taste with salt and pepper and whisk with a balloon whisk or fork until thoroughly blended.

Put the turnips and onion slices in a serving bowl. Season with coarse sea salt and pepper. Pour over the dressing and toss well. Serve warm, sprinkled with roughly torn parsley.

WARM BABY TURNIPS WITH SWEET MUSTARD DRESSING

RAINBOW TROUT WITH SOURED CREAM & HORSERADISH

TAKES 40–45 MINS
SERVES 4

150 g/5 oz butter

125 g/4 oz blanched almonds, toasted and chopped

125 g/4 oz fresh white breadcrumbs

juice and finely grated rind of 1 lemon

4 x 375 g/12 oz rainbow trout, cleaned

salt and pepper

HORSERADISH SAUCE

125 ml/4 fl oz soured cream

4 teaspoons grated horseradish

4 tablespoons chopped parsley

2 tablespoons chopped mint

Make the horseradish sauce. Put the soured cream, horseradish, parsley and mint in a food processor or blender. Whizz until smooth, then turn into a bowl, season to taste with salt and pepper and set aside.

Melt 125 g/4 oz butter in a small saucepan, add the chopped almonds, breadcrumbs, lemon rind and juice, and salt and pepper. Mix well, stuff into the trout cavities, then reshape the fish.

Brush each trout lightly with the remaining butter. Cook under a moderately hot grill, turning once, for 5–10 minutes or until the fish comes away from the bone. Serve immediately with the horseradish sauce.

RHUBARB

YOU MIGHT BE SURPRISED TO KNOW THAT RHUBARB IS ACTUALLY A VEGETABLE, ALTHOUGH ITS UNIQUE FLAVOUR IS USED MORE OFTEN IN SWEET PIES, CRUMBLES AND TARTS. RHUBARB ORIGINALLY CAME FROM ASIA AND SIBERIA OVER 2,000 YEARS AGO, WHERE IT WAS USED FOR MEDICINAL RATHER THAN CULINARY PURPOSES. IT CAME TO BRITAIN IN THE 17TH CENTURY, AND UNTIL A DECADE OR SO AGO EVERY BACK GARDEN OR YARD HAD A RHUBARB PLANT, AND IT WAS SEEN AS A BREATH OF FRESH AIR ON THE DINNER TABLE AFTER MONTHS OF EATING ROOT VEGETABLES. ITS POPULARITY DIDN'T LAST, AND IT IS ONLY FAIRLY RECENTLY THAT THERE HAS BEEN A RHUBARB REVIVAL. SADLY, IT SEEMS IT COULD BE UNDER THREAT AGAIN AS IT IS NOT SUITED TO THE WARMER CLIMATE THAT MANY GARDENERS HAVE BEEN EXPERIENCING LATELY.

GOOD FOR YOU

Rhubarb contains vitamins C and E. It is a good source of fibre, which is thought to help reduce cholesterol levels. It also contains potassium, manganese and calcium. Rhubarb is thought to aid weight loss as it is low in carbohydrate and can be a useful addition to a GI diet, as long as it isn't accompanied by too much sugar.

FIVE OF THE BEST

Champagne This is an early cultivar, which has very sweet, pink-edged stems.

Timperley Early A popular cultivar, this is good for forcing and for normal cropping. It has pink stems and a good flavour.

Victoria This classic allotment rhubarb forces well and produces juicy stems.

Ace of Hearts This is the ideal cultivar for growing in a small space.

Prince Albert This is an early producer, with long stems.

DELICIOUS IDEAS TO TRY

Compôte Cut 500 g/1 lb of rhubarb into 5 cm/2 inch lengths. Add to a saucepan with 150 g/5 oz caster sugar, the seeds of a vanilla pod, a dash of white wine and a little water. Simmer over a low heat until stewed.

Sorbet Purée your rhubarb compôte in a blender then freeze in a container. Serve with some chopped mint.

Roast Sprinkle rhubarb stems with brown sugar and add some freshly squeezed orange juice. Bake until tender in a moderately hot oven. Serve with cream or custard.

Breakfast Serve rhubarb compôte with natural yogurt and muesli for a healthy breakfast.

Sweet and sour Use any leftover puréed compôte to serve with cold meats, such as finely sliced duck or chicken, or with mackerel.

TOP TIPS FOR RHUBARB

Never eat rhubarb leaves because they contain oxalic acid, which is poisonous.

Rhubarb wilts quickly, so once picked it should be stored in the refrigerator and eaten quickly.

To freeze rhubarb, wash and trim the stems and cut them into 2.5 cm/1 inch lengths. Freeze 500 g/1 lb in polythene bags. Cook from frozen.

TAKES 50–55 MINS
SERVES 4

400 g/13 oz rhubarb, trimmed and thinly sliced

1 ripe pear, peeled, cored and sliced

100 g/3^{1}/$_{2}$ oz caster sugar

125 g/4 oz plain flour

50 g/2 oz unsalted butter, cut into pieces

125 g/4 oz marzipan, coarsely grated

flaked almonds, for sprinkling

custard, to serve

🍃 Put the rhubarb and pear into a 1.2 litre/ 2 pint ovenproof pie dish with half the sugar.

🍃 Put the rest of the sugar into a food processor, add the flour and butter and whizz until the mixture resembles fine breadcrumbs. Alternatively, put the ingredients into a mixing bowl and rub in the butter with your fingertips. Stir in the grated marzipan.

🍃 Spoon the crumble mixture over the fruit and sprinkle with a few flaked almonds. Cook in a preheated oven, 180°C/350°F/Gas Mark 4, for 35–40 minutes until golden brown, checking after 15–20 minutes and covering with foil if necessary. Serve immediately with custard.

RHUBARB, PEAR & MARZIPAN CRUMBLE

THE GOOD

RHUBARB, APPLE & DOUBLE GINGER CRUMBLE

TAKES 1 HR 10 MINS
SERVES 8

125 g/4 oz plain flour

50 g/2 oz ginger biscuits, crushed

25 g/1 oz porridge oats

75 g/3 oz unsalted butter, plus
extra for greasing

3 tablespoons light muscovado sugar

500 g/1 lb rhubarb, trimmed and sliced

2 tablespoons chopped preserved stem ginger,
plus 2 tablespoons ginger syrup from jar

50 g/2 oz caster sugar

4 tablespoons water

375 g/12 oz dessert apples, peeled,
cored and sliced

15 g/¹/₂ oz unsalted butter

Sift the flour into a bowl and stir in the crushed biscuits and oats. Rub in the butter with your fingertips until the mixture resembles breadcrumbs. Stir in the muscovado sugar.

Put the rhubarb in a saucepan with the chopped ginger, ginger syrup, caster sugar and measured water. Heat gently, cover and simmer for 10 minutes.

Put the sliced apples in a greased pie dish. Add the rhubarb and butter and sprinkle over the crumble topping. Bake in a preheated oven, 190°C/375°F/ Gas Mark 5, for 40 minutes until bubbling and the topping is golden. Serve hot or warm.

LIFE

OLD-FASHIONED RHUBARB PIE

TAKES 55–60 MINS
SERVES 6–8

PASTRY

250 g/8 oz plain flour

125 g/4 oz chilled unsalted butter, diced

25 g/1 oz caster sugar

1 egg yolk

1 egg white, lightly beaten, to glaze

caster sugar, for dredging

FILLING

750 g/1 ½ lb rhubarb, trimmed and sliced

25 g/1 oz unsalted butter

50 g/2 oz light muscovado sugar

Make the pastry. Put the flour in a bowl. Add the butter and rub in with your fingertips until the mixture resembles fine breadcrumbs. Stir in the sugar, then add the egg yolk and enough cold water, 3–4 tablespoons, to mix to a firm dough.

Turn the dough out on a lightly floured surface and knead briefly. Roll out to a round about 35 cm/14 inches across. Lift the round on to a 23 cm/9 inch pie plate. Fill the centre of the pie with the rhubarb, dot with the butter and sprinkle with the muscovado sugar. Fold the overlapping pastry over the filling; some of the filling will still show.

Brush the top of the pastry with egg white and dredge with caster sugar. Bake in a preheated oven, 200°C/400°F/Gas Mark 6, for 35–40 minutes until the pastry is golden brown. Serve warm.

Put two-thirds of the rhubarb into a large pan and mix in the ginger, orange rind and the juice from the lemons, then add the orange juice and measured water. Chop the lemon shells, tie the pieces securely in a piece of clean muslin and add to the pan. Bring the mixture to the boil, reduce the heat and simmer steadily, uncovered, for about 1 hour. The fruit should be reduced by half at the end of the simmering time.

Allow the fruit to cool, then remove the muslin and squeeze out all the juices from it into the pan. Add the remaining rhubarb, return the jam to the boil and simmer for 5–10 minutes, until the fruit is soft. Gradually stir in the sugar and continue stirring over a low heat until the sugar has completely dissolved. Bring the jam to the boil once more and boil hard until it reaches setting point. Remove the pan from the heat and carefully skim off any scum.

Transfer the jam to warm, dry jars. Cover the surface of each with a disc of waxed paper, waxed side down, then top with an airtight lid or cellophane cover. Label and leave to cool, then store in a cool, dark place. It will keep for 3–4 months.

TAKES 2 HRS, PLUS COOLING
MAKES 2.75–3.25 KG/6–7 LB

1.5 kg/3 lb rhubarb, trimmed and sliced

50 g/2 oz fresh root ginger, peeled and finely sliced

juice and chopped, pared rind of 2 oranges

2 lemons, halved

1.2 litres/2 pints water

1.75 kg/3½ lb sugar

RHUBARB, ORANGE & GINGER JAM

GARLIC HERBS SPINACH MIXED
LEAVES LETTUCE ROCKET SWEET
POTATO GREEN BEANS PEAS BROAD
BEANS TOMATOES AUBERGINES
POTATOES ARTICHOKES PLUMS
RASPBERRIES BLACKCURRANTS
REDCURRANTS ELDERFLOWERS
GOOSEBERRIES

FARE

IN SUMMER

The summer season brings prolific growth in the kitchen garden: vegetables and fruit are abundant, varied and delicious. Crisp salad leaves and tomatoes will be plentiful, and can be enjoyed with new potatoes and green beans. Summer is all about easy cooking with simple recipes to enjoy al fresco – barbecues with potato salad, griddled tomatoes and mixed leaf salads with herbs. Remember that the most important job in the allotment is the watering – all your fruit and vegetables will need a good soaking when the sun has gone down. Don't forget to pinch out the sideshoots on your tomatoes and watch out for aphids. Make the most of the longer, warmer days by sowing beetroot and carrot seeds, and start thinking about stocking up your freezer with plums, gooseberries, green beans and peas as they come into season.

MAKE THE MOST OF ...

AUBERGINES

Aubergines can be grown in grow bags in a greenhouse, and some of the new cultivars are suitable for growing in containers. They have similar requirements to tomatoes. Harvest them when the aubergine is a good size and colour. The skin should be shiny and bright. Fresh aubergines can be stored in a refrigerator for about a week.

BROAD BEANS

Harvest broad beans from the bottom of the plant to the top, cutting them off with scissors. The beans should be small but plump, sweet and tasty, but don't leave them or they will become tough and bitter. Eat broad beans fresh or blanch and freeze them.

GREEN BEANS

Green beans are useful plants, because not only do they taste good but they are also attractive. If you harvest your crop on a regular basis you will prolong the season. A pod at its peak should snap in half and be crunchy. Young pods are best eaten while they are fresh, but they can also be blanched and frozen. The haricot beans of mature pods can be dried and stored in an airtight container.

GOOSEBERRIES

Harvest half the crop in early summer because this will prolong the season and mean that the remaining gooseberries will grow bigger and be full of flavour. The gooseberries should be tender and plump. It is better to cook them with some sugar before freezing or use them fresh in pies, tarts and fools.

NEW POTATOES

New potatoes start to appear in late spring, but they really come into their own throughout the summer months. Lift the first crop on a dry day. Check that all the flowers are open on the plant and carefully dig up the tubers with a garden fork, taking care not to damage the potatoes. Leave them spread out on the path for a couple of hours to dry. They can be stored in potato sacks in a cool, dry place and should keep for several months.

PEAS

Peas need to be harvested regularly when the pods are at their peak, so that the peas are really fresh. Remove any pods that have gone over so that they don't sap nutrients from the plant. Harvest from the bottom to the top of the plant. Eat the peas immediately or freeze them. You can also use the sideshoots in salads.

PLUMS

Leave the plums on the tree until they are ripe, then taste them to see if they are ready: they should be sweet and juicy and the stone should come away from the fruit easily. Plums can be stored in a cool, dry, airy room in crates for several weeks. If you have a glut you can pickle them or make plum jam. Cook the plums with sugar if you want to freeze them.

SALAD LEAVES

Salad leaves are one of the easiest crops to grow, and even if you don't have much space you can grow some mixed leaves in a container or windowbox. Cut the leaves rather than pull them up so

that the plant will reshoot – these are often known as cut-and-come-again plants. Put the leaves into cold water to prevent them from wilting, rinse and store in a bag in the refrigerator for a few days.

SPINACH

Spinach is such a versatile leaf that it's surprising it's not more widely grown. It's delicious in salads and also in cooked dishes. Remember to sow seed in succession so that you can pick fresh leaves over several months. Harvest before the plants bolt. Rinse and store the leaves in plastic bags in the refrigerator.

STRAWBERRIES

Strawberries should be picked as soon as they are ripe – otherwise they will rot on the plant or be eaten by slugs and snails. Pick at least every other day to get the best out of the fruit and make sure that the green stalk stays intact on the strawberry. If you have too many, try making some jam or flavouring vinegar.

GARLIC BRUSCHETTA

TAKES 10 MINS
SERVES 4

8 slices of ciabatta bread

2 garlic cloves, peeled

small handful of flat leaf parsley, chopped

5 tablespoons olive oil

salt

Toast the slices of bread under a preheated grill until golden-brown.

Rub the garlic over one side of the bread; the bread acts as a grater and the garlic will be evenly spread over the slices of bread.

Sprinkle the bruschetta with the parsley and salt to taste and drizzle with the oil. Serve immediately or keep warm until required, but do not keep warm for too long or the bruschetta will lose its crunchiness.

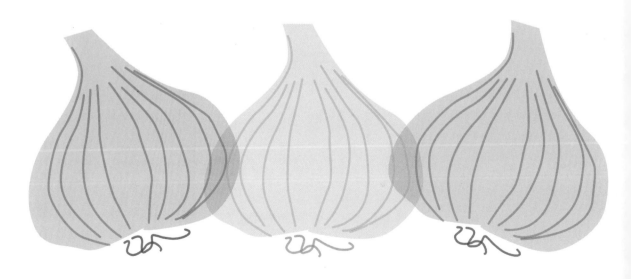

TAKES 15 MINS, PLUS SOAKING AND CHILLING
SERVES 6

50 g/2 oz bread

125 g/4 oz raisins

125 g/4 oz blanched almonds, toasted

3 tablespoons olive oil

3 garlic cloves, crushed or roughly chopped

900 ml/1 1/2 pints milk or water

hyssop flowers or borage flowers, to garnish

Roughly tear the bread into small pieces and put them in a small bowl. Put the raisins in a separate bowl and cover both the bread and raisins with water. Leave to soak for 30–60 minutes or until the raisins are plump.

Remove the bread from the water and squeeze to remove the excess moisture. Put the bread in a blender or food processor, add the almonds and whizz to make a smooth paste.

Add the oil, garlic, raisins and milk or water and whizz again until smooth.

Cover the soup and chill in the refrigerator for 2–3 hours to allow the flavours to mingle. Serve in small soup bowls topped with hyssop or borage flowers.

GARLIC & ALMOND SOUP

Put the measured water, vinegar, sugar and salt in a large saucepan, bring to the boil, then reduce the heat and simmer for 5 minutes.

Add the garlic to the pan, return to the boil and boil hard for 1 minute.

Remove the pan from the heat, allow the garlic mixture to cool, then transfer to containers and top with airtight lids. Label and leave to mature in the refrigerator for 10 days before using or store, unopened, for 6 months.

TAKES 40 MINS, PLUS COOLING
MAKES 6 GARLIC HEADS

1.2 litres/2 pints water

300 ml/½ pint distilled white wine vinegar

50 g/2 oz granulated sugar

1 tablespoon salt

6 heads of garlic, separated into cloves and peeled

PICKLED GARLIC

DIG FOR YO

GARLIC PRAWN TAPAS

TAKES 30 MINS
SERVES 4

2 garlic cloves, crushed

1 teaspoon paprika

**1 medium-hot red chilli,
deseeded and finely chopped**

2 tablespoons olive oil

**500 g/1 lb large whole
raw prawns**

salt

AIOLI

4–6 garlic cloves, crushed

¹/₂ teaspoon salt

2 egg yolks

1 tablespoon lemon juice

300 ml/¹/₂ pint light olive oil

salt and pepper

Make the aïoli. Put the garlic, salt, egg yolks and lemon juice in a food processor or blender and whizz for 1 minute. With the motor running, pour the oil through the feeder tube in a steady stream until the sauce is thick and glossy. Thin down with a little boiling water if necessary, and season to taste with salt and pepper. Transfer to a bowl and set aside.

Mix together the garlic, paprika, chilli, oil and a little salt in a large bowl. (If you're preparing this in advance, leave the salt until you're ready to cook.) Add the prawns and toss them in the mixture until they are evenly coated.

Heat a ridged grill pan or heavy-based frying pan and add half the prawns, spreading them in a single layer. Cook for 2–3 minutes or until they are deep pink on the underside. Turn and cook for a further 1–2 minutes. Transfer to a warm dish and cook the remainder in the same way. Serve immediately with the Aïoli.

HERBS

HERBS HAVE BEEN GROWN FOR THOUSANDS OF YEARS. THE ROMANS INTRODUCED THEM TO BRITAIN, AND THEIR PRIMARY USES WERE IN MEDICINES AND TOILETRIES. THEN THEY WERE USED FOR FLAVOURING FOODS, ALTHOUGH PROBABLY AT FIRST THEY WERE USED MORE TO DISGUISE THE TASTES AND SMELLS THAN TO ENHANCE THEM. LUCKILY, MANY OF THE HERBS THAT WERE NATIVE TO MEDITERRANEAN COUNTRIES SURVIVED THE HARSHER CONDITIONS OF NORTHERN EUROPE, AND THEY HAVE BECOME AN ESSENTIAL ELEMENT IN MOST GARDENS. THE 17TH-CENTURY PHYSICIAN NICHOLAS CULPEPER ENSURED THEIR POPULARITY WITH HIS WRITINGS, AND TODAY NO ALLOTMENT OR GARDEN WOULD BE COMPLETE WITHOUT A SELECTION OF HERBS. NOT ONLY ARE THEY AN ESSENTIAL PART OF THE WAY WE COOK, BUT THEY ARE AN ATTRACTIVE ADDITION TO ANY GROWING SPACE.

GOOD FOR YOU

Journals dating from about 3000 BC describe the healing properties of herbs, but many herbs are also rich in vitamins, minerals and antioxidants and therefore play an important part in healthy eating. As part of a balanced diet they can help prolong good health, help delay the ageing process and help protect against many diseases.

FIVE OF THE BEST

Basil This is a great annual herb to grow in a pot with some tomatoes in a sunny spot. It is a key ingredient in Italian dishes.

Mint Probably the most fragrant of all the herbs, there are several types, with different flavours and leaf colours. Plant mint in a container in a bed to prevent the roots from spreading. It's fantastic with tomatoes and is a perfect partner to lamb.

Chives This hardy herb can reward you nearly all year round, and its beautiful flowers are a great addition to salads.

Thyme A compact and easy plant to grow, thyme has attractive foliage and flowers. You can add the leaves, fresh or dried, to stews, stocks and pizzas.

French tarragon With its sweet aniseed scent, this herb makes a great addition to creamy sauces, chicken dishes and fish.

DELICIOUS IDEAS TO TRY

Butter Combine 175 g/6 oz softened butter with 5 tablespoons mixed herbs, such as parsley, tarragon, thyme and chives, some chopped garlic and salt and pepper. Store in clingfilm or foil in the freezer in 50 g/2 oz pats. Serve with fish, potatoes, bread or steak.

Tisanes Crush a sprig or 5 leaves of your chosen herb and add to a cup of boiling water. Infuse for 5 minutes then remove the herb. Mint and camomile are popular choices, but you can try other leaves.

Salad Try a salad of mixed green leaves, mixed herbs, such as coriander, mint and basil, and avocado and cherry tomatoes. Drizzle with lemon juice and olive oil.

Pesto Place 2 handfuls of basil leaves, 1 garlic clove, 25 g/1 oz pine nuts, 75 g/3 oz grated Parmesan cheese and 150 ml/¼ pint olive oil and whizz in a food processor until smooth. Serve with hot pasta.

Stuffing Add sage or tarragon to fresh breadcrumbs, a chopped, fried onion, lemon rind and a beaten egg.

TOP TIPS FOR HERBS

Site in a sunny position in well-drained soil and water regularly.

To contain spreading roots, plant in a pot and then into a herb bed.

Make sure you have herbs all year round by chopping them finely and adding them to ice cube trays with a little water. Freeze and use when needed.

MEDITERRANEAN HERB OIL

TAKES 15 MINS, PLUS STANDING
MAKES 2 X 500 ML/17 FL OZ BOTTLES

large handful of mixed herbs, including rosemary, thyme and marjoram, or a single variety, such as rosemary, tarragon or thyme

1 litre/1 ³/₄ pints olive oil

extra herbs, to finish

Put the herbs into a large, clean, dry, wide-necked storage jar and top up with the oil.

Seal tightly and turn the jar upside down several times to bruise the leaves slightly and to release their flavouring oils.

Leave the jar in a warm place for 2 weeks, turning it once a day.

Strain the oil through a fine sieve to remove all sediment, then transfer the oil to dry bottles and tuck a few herb sprigs into the bottles to decorate. Seal with airtight tops, then label clearly and store in a cool, dark place. The oil will keep for up to 6 months.

Heat the stock in a saucepan to a gentle simmer.

Melt 50 g/2 oz butter with the oil in a saucepan. Add the onion and garlic and sauté for 3 minutes.

Add the rice, stir well to coat the grains with the butter and oil, then add a ladleful of stock, enough to cover the rice, and stir well. Simmer gently and continue to stir as frequently as possible, adding more stock as it is absorbed. Continue adding the stock and stirring until it has all been absorbed and the rice is cooked with a rich creamy sauce.

Add the herbs, the remaining butter and the cheese. Season with salt and pepper and stir well. Serve immediately, garnished with the herb sprigs.

GREEN HERB RISOTTO

TAKES 30 MINS
SERVES 4

1 litre/1³/₄ pints chicken or vegetable stock

125 g/4 oz butter

2 tablespoons olive oil

1 onion, finely chopped

1 garlic clove, crushed and chopped

300 g/10 oz arborio or carnaroli rice

handful of parsley, chopped

handful of basil, chopped

handful of oregano, chopped

handful of thyme, chopped

125 g/4 oz Toma cheese, grated

salt and pepper

herb sprigs, to garnish

TAKES 25–27 MINS
SERVES 4

3 tablespoons chopped parsley

1 tablespoon chopped tarragon

2 tablespoons chopped basil

1 tablespoon olive oil

1 large garlic clove, crushed

4 tablespoons vegetable stock

2 tablespoons dry white wine

375 g/12 oz dried spaghetti

salt and pepper

SPAGHETTI WITH THREE HERB SAUCE

🌿 Put the parsley, tarragon, basil, oil, garlic, stock and wine in a food processor and whizz until smooth. Season to taste with salt and pepper.

🌿 Cook the spaghetti in a large saucepan of lightly salted boiling water for 10–12 minutes or according to the instructions on the packet until it is just tender.

🌿 Drain the spaghetti and pile it into a warm bowl. Pour over the herb sauce and toss well to mix, then serve immediately.

THE GOOD

HERB OMELETTE WITH MUSTARD MUSHROOMS

TAKES 15 MINS
SERVES 2

1 tablespoon wholegrain mustard

50 g/2 oz butter, softened

4 flat mushrooms

2 tablespoons chopped mixed herbs, such as chives, parsley and tarragon

4 eggs

salt and pepper

 Beat the mustard into 40 g/1½ oz butter and spread it over the undersides of the mushrooms. Place them on a foil-lined grill pan and cook for 5–6 minutes until golden and tender. Remove and keep warm.

 Meanwhile, beat the herbs into the eggs and season to taste with salt and pepper.

 Melt the remaining butter in an omelette or nonstick frying pan, swirl in the egg mixture and cook until almost set. Carefully slide the omelette and flip it over on to a warm plate, add the mushrooms and serve immediately.

LIFE

HERB SALAD WITH GRILLED HALOUMI

1 cos lettuce

about 50 g/2 oz rocket or young leaf spinach

handful of mixed herbs, roughly torn, such as dill, chervil, coriander, basil and parsley

250 g/8 oz haloumi cheese

1–2 tablespoons olive oil

freshly ground black pepper

FRENCH DRESSING

2 tablespoons red or white wine vinegar

1–2 garlic cloves, crushed

2 teaspoons Dijon mustard

¼ teaspoon caster sugar

6 tablespoons olive oil

salt and pepper

Make the dressing. Mix together the vinegar, garlic, mustard and sugar in a small bowl. Add salt and pepper to taste and stir well. Gradually whisk in the olive oil. Taste and add more salt and pepper if necessary.

Tear the lettuce leaves into bite-sized pieces and place them in a large, shallow salad bowl with the rocket or leaf spinach and mixed herbs.

Cut the cheese into small dice and put them in a baking tin large enough to hold them in a single layer. Add the olive oil and season with pepper. Toss gently to coat the cheese and grill under a preheated hot grill, stirring occasionally, for about 8 minutes until golden brown on all sides.

Add the dressing to the salad and toss well, scatter over the grilled cheese and serve immediately.

Pat the cod fillets dry with kitchen paper and season to taste with salt and pepper. Put the fish, skin side down, in a foil-lined roasting tin.

Make the herb crust. Mix together the remaining ingredients in a bowl and spoon some on top of each cod fillet, packing the mixture down gently.

Cook the cod fillets in a preheated oven, 180°C/350°F, Gas Mark 4, for 20 minutes, covering the tin with foil if the crust is getting too brown. Serve with whole green beans and tagliatelle.

TAKES 35 MINS
SERVES 4

4 cod fillets, each about 125 g/4 oz

50 g/2 oz wholemeal breadcrumbs

2 tablespoons chopped dill

2 tablespoons chopped parsley

2 tablespoons snipped chives

2 tablespoons fromage frais

2 plum tomatoes, finely diced

2 tablespoons lemon juice

salt and pepper

TO SERVE

green beans

tagliatelle

COD FILLETS WITH A HERB CRUST

TAKES 55 MINS
SERVES 4–6

25 g/1 oz butter

40 g/1 ½ oz plain flour

1 teaspoon Dijon mustard

200 ml/7 fl oz semi-skimmed milk

50 g/2 oz vegetarian cheese, grated

4 eggs, separated

4 tablespoons chopped mixed herbs, such as basil, chervil, chives, tarragon and thyme

salt and pepper

FILLING

175 g/6 oz ricotta or curd cheese

2 tablespoons olive oil, plus extra for oiling

pinch of grated nutmeg

1 leek, finely chopped

500 g/1 lb frozen leaf spinach, thawed, drained and squeezed

¼ teaspoon grated nutmeg

Tomato Sauce (see page 105), to serve

Grease and line a 23 x 33 cm/9 x 13 inch Swiss roll tin. Melt the butter in a saucepan, add the flour and mustard and cook over a low heat for 1 minute. Gradually add the milk, stirring. Bring the sauce slowly to the boil, stirring constantly until the sauce thickens. Cook over a gentle heat for 2 minutes.

Remove the pan from the heat and allow the sauce to cool slightly. Beat in the cheese, egg yolks and herbs. Season to taste with salt and pepper. Whisk the egg whites until stiff and fold into the sauce until evenly incorporated.

Pour the mixture into the prepared tin and cook in a preheated oven, 200°C/400°F, Gas Mark 6, for 12–15 minutes until risen and firm to the touch. Remove from the oven and leave to cool. Reduce the oven temperature to 190°C/375°F, Gas Mark 5.

Meanwhile, prepare the filling. Cream the cheese and half the oil together and season with nutmeg, salt and pepper.

Heat the remaining oil in a frying pan. Fry the leeks for 5 minutes. Finely chop the spinach, add to the pan and cook gently for 5 minutes.

Turn the roulade out of the tin and carefully peel away the paper. Spread over the softened cheese and then the spinach mixture. Roll up from a short end and place on the oiled baking sheet. Brush with oil and cook for 20–25 minutes. Serve hot in slices, with tomato sauce.

HERB ROULADE WITH SPINACH & RICOTTA

PASTA BAKE WITH SPINACH & HAM

TAKES 30 MINS
SERVES 4

2 tablespoons olive oil

1 onion, chopped

1 garlic clove, crushed and chopped

750 g/1 ½ lb spinach, washed, drained and chopped

pinch of grated nutmeg

8 sheets fresh lasagne

250 g/8 oz ham, chopped into large chunks

125 g/4 oz packet buffalo mozzarella cheese, thinly sliced

125 g/4 oz fontina cheese, grated

salt and pepper

🍃 Heat the olive oil in a saucepan. Add the onion and garlic and sauté for 3 minutes.

🍃 Add the spinach and mix well, cook for 2 minutes over a moderate heat, until the spinach starts to wilt. Add nutmeg to taste and season with salt and pepper.

🍃 Lightly oil a large, shallow baking dish. Put a layer of lasagne in the base, followed by a layer of spinach, then some ham and then a layer of mozzarella. Repeat the layering until all the ingredients are used, finishing with lasagne and the grated fontina.

🍃 Put the lasagne at the top of a preheated oven, 200°C/400°F, Gas Mark 6, and cook for 15 minutes until golden brown and bubbling. Serve immediately.

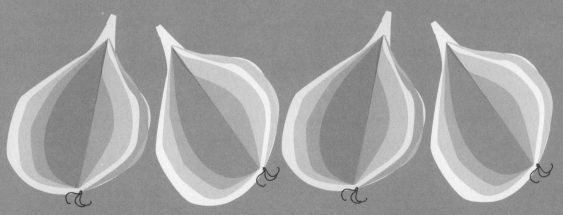

Put the lasagne in a large roasting tin and cover with boiling water. Leave to stand for 5 minutes or until tender, then drain thoroughly.

Meanwhile, heat the oil in a large frying pan. Fry the mushrooms for 5 minutes, add the mascarpone and turn up the heat. Cook for 1 minute until the sauce is thick. Season with salt and pepper.

Lightly oil an ovenproof dish and arrange 3 sheets of lasagne in the base, slightly overlapping. Top with a little of the Taleggio, one-third of the mushroom sauce and one-third of the spinach leaves. Repeat with 2 more layers, then top the final layer of lasagne with the remaining Taleggio.

Cook the lasagne under a preheated hot grill for 5 minutes until the cheese is bubbling and golden. Serve immediately.

TAKES 26 MINS
SERVES 4

12 sheets fresh lasagne

3 tablespoons olive oil

500 g/1 lb mixed mushrooms, such as shiitake, oyster and chestnut, sliced

200 g/7 oz mascarpone cheese

125 g/4 oz baby spinach

150 g/5 oz Taleggio cheese, derinded and diced

salt and pepper

QUICK MUSHROOM & SPINACH LASAGNE

GNOCCHI WITH SPINACH & THREE CHEESE SAUCE

TAKES 20–21 MINS
SERVES 4

500 g/1 lb ready-made gnocchi

250 g/8 oz frozen leaf spinach, thawed

250 g/8 oz mascarpone cheese

50 g/2 oz dolcelatte cheese

pinch of grated nutmeg

2 tablespoons grated Parmesan cheese

salt and pepper

Cook the gnocchi in a large saucepan of lightly salted boiling water according to the instructions on the packet. Drain well and return them to the pan.

Meanwhile, drain the spinach. Use your hands to squeeze out all the excess water and chop the leaves roughly.

Stir the spinach into the cooked gnocchi with the mascarpone, dolcelatte and a little grated nutmeg. Stir gently until creamy and season with salt and pepper.

Spoon the mixture into a shallow heatproof dish, sprinkle over the Parmesan and cook under a preheated hot grill for 5–6 minutes until bubbling and golden.

280 g/8¹/₂ oz packet pizza
base mix

1 tablespoon olive oil

1 garlic clove, crushed

2 sprigs of rosemary, chopped

200 g/7 oz frozen spinach,
thawed

125 g/4 oz dolcelatte cheese

4 tablespoons mascarpone
cheese

pinch of grated nutmeg

150 g/5 oz mozzarella
cheese, sliced

25 g/1 oz Parmesan
cheese, grated

salt and pepper

Put 2 baking sheets into a preheated oven, 220°C/425°F,
Gas Mark 7, to heat up.

Make up the pizza dough with the olive oil, according to the
instructions on the packet, adding the garlic and rosemary to the
mix. Divide the dough in half and roll out each piece to a round
about 35 cm/14 inches across.

Use your hands to squeeze out all the excess liquid from the
spinach. Chop the leaves and beat in the dolcelatte, mascarpone and
grated nutmeg. Season to taste with salt and pepper.

Put a pizza base on a well-floured board and top with half the
spinach mixture, half the mozzarella and half the Parmesan. Season to
taste with salt and pepper. Carefully slide the pizza on to a heated
baking sheet. Repeat to make the second pizza and transfer it to the
second baking sheet.

Cook the pizzas for 12 minutes, swapping their position halfway
through cooking so that they brown evenly. Cut each pizza in half
and serve immediately.

SPINACH
& FOUR
CHEESE
PIZZA

CHICKEN & SPINACH MASALA

TAKES 30–35 MINS
SERVES 4

2 tablespoons vegetable oil

I onion, thinly sliced

2 garlic cloves, crushed

I green chilli, deseeded and thinly sliced

I teaspoon fresh root ginger, finely grated

I teaspoon ground coriander

I teaspoon ground cumin

200 g/7 oz can tomatoes

750 g/1¾ lb boneless chicken thighs, skinned and cut into bite-sized chunks

200 ml/7 fl oz crème fraîche

300 g/10 oz spinach, washed, drained and roughly chopped

2 tablespoons chopped coriander leaves

salt and pepper

naan bread or boiled rice, to serve

Heat the oil in a large heavy-based saucepan. Add the onion, garlic, chilli and ginger; stir-fry for 2–3 minutes and then add the ground coriander and cumin. Stir and cook for 1 minute.

Pour in the tomatoes with their juice and cook gently for 3 minutes. Increase the heat and add the chicken thighs. Cook, stirring, until the outside of the chicken is sealed. Then stir in the crème fraîche and spinach.

Cover the pan and cook the chicken mixture gently for 6–8 minutes, stirring occasionally. Stir in the coriander and season to taste with salt and pepper. Serve hot with naan bread or boiled basmati rice.

SPICED SPINACH & CARROT PANCAKES

TAKES 30 MINS
MAKES 6

75 g/3 oz carrots, grated

75 g/3 oz spinach, roughly chopped

I onion, finely chopped

2 fresh green chillies, deseeded and chopped

I teaspoon fennel seeds

I tablespoon ground coriander

I00 g/3¹/₂ oz gram flour (besan), sieved

50 g/2 oz semolina

I teaspoon baking powder

300 ml/¹/₂ pint water

vegetable oil, for oiling

sea salt

Minty Yogurt (see page II3), to serve

Mix together the carrots, spinach, onion, chillies, fennel seeds and coriander in a large bowl. Season to taste with salt and set aside.

Mix together the gram flour, semolina and baking powder and add to the carrot mixture.

Gradually add the measured water to the mixture, mixing well with a spoon, until you have a thick batter.

Lightly oil a nonstick frying pan and heat the pan. Add 2 tablespoons of the mixture to the pan and spread it with a spatula to make a pancake 17–18 cm/ 6½–7 inches across. Cover and cook for 1–2 minutes or until the pancake is lightly browned on the base. Flip over and cook for another 2 minutes. Repeat with the remaining batter to make 6 pancakes.

Serve the pancakes hot with the minty yogurt dip.

Heat half the oil in a nonstick frying pan. Add the onion and cook until softened. Add the cumin, turmeric and chilli flakes and cook, stirring, for 1 minute. Add the lentils, spinach and crème fraîche and cook gently for about 5 minutes until the spinach has wilted.

Meanwhile, brush the fish fillets on each side with the remaining oil. Arrange the haddock on a nonstick baking sheet and cook under a preheated hot grill for 2–3 minutes on each side until just cooked through.

Arrange the lentils and spinach mixture on warm serving plates and top each one with a haddock fillet. Garnish with a lemon wedge and serve with grilled tomatoes.

GRILLED HADDOCK WITH LENTILS & SPINACH

TAKES 30 MINS
SERVES 2

2 teaspoons olive oil

1 onion, finely chopped

pinch of ground cumin

pinch of ground turmeric

pinch of dried red chilli flakes

250 g/8 oz can lentils, drained and rinsed

175 g/6 oz baby spinach leaves

4 tablespoons crème fraîche

2 skinless haddock fillets, each about 125 g/4 oz

lemon wedges, to garnish

grilled tomatoes, to serve

Wash the leaves and discard the thick stems from the spinach and chard. Transfer the wet leaves to a large pan and cook gently, stirring, until the leaves have wilted. Strain off as much excess liquid as possible, then return the leaves to the pan.

Stir in the oil, garlic and lemon juice. Season to taste with salt and pepper. Heat gently for 2–3 minutes, or until the greens are tender.

Meanwhile, toast the bread and poach the eggs. Put a slice of toast on each of 4 serving plates, top with a pile of greens, then a poached egg. Serve immediately.

POACHED EGGS & MIXED LEAVES WITH LEMON OIL

TAKES 20 MINS
SERVES 4

1 kg/2 lb mixed salad leaves, such as spinach, rocket and chard

4 tablespoons olive oil

1 garlic clove, crushed

2 tablespoons lemon juice

salt and pepper

4 slices of wholemeal bread

4 eggs

MIXED LEAF & POMEGRANATE SALAD

TAKES 10 MINS
SERVES 6

3 tablespoons raspberry vinegar

2 tablespoons light olive oil

1 pomegranate

125 g/4 oz mixed salad leaves, including baby spinach leaves, red mustard and mizuna

salt and pepper

raspberries, to garnish (optional)

Put the raspberry vinegar, olive oil and a little salt and pepper in a salad bowl and mix together lightly.

Cut the pomegranate in half and again into large pieces. Flex the skin so that the small red seeds fall out. Pick out any stubborn ones with a small knife and discard, then add the remainder to the salad bowl, discarding the skin and pith.

Tear any large salad leaves into bite-sized pieces and toss all the leaves in the dressing. Sprinkle with raspberries (if used) and serve immediately.

1 cooked crab, about 500 g/1 lb,
cleaned

4 small iceberg lettuce leaves

salt and pepper

RELISH

¹/₄ cucumber, finely diced

3 red spring onions, thinly sliced

¹/₂ large red chilli, deseeded and
finely chopped

2 tablespoons white wine vinegar

1 teaspoon light soy sauce

1 teaspoon caster sugar

4 teaspoons finely chopped mint
or coriander

🍃 Make the relish. Mix all the ingredients in a bowl with a little salt
and pepper.

🍃 Twist and remove the 2 large claws and spider-like legs from the
crab and set aside. With the crab upside down, pull away the ball-like,
spongy lungs. Check that the small sac and any green matter have
been removed, then scoop the brown meat and skin from under
the shell on to a plate. Break up the crabmeat with a spoon.

🍃 Put the crab claws in a plastic bag, hit them once or twice with
a rolling pin or meat mallet to break the shells, then, working on one
at a time, peel away the shell, removing the white flesh with a small
knife and a skewer. Add to the brown crabmeat.

🍃 When you are ready to serve, spoon the crab into the lettuce
leaves and top with spoonfuls of the cucumber relish. Roll up the
leaves and eat with your fingers.

LETTUCE WRAPPERS WITH CRAB & CUCUMBER RELISH

BRESAOLA WITH RICOTTA & ROCKET

TAKES 10 MINS
SERVES 4 AS A STARTER

20 slices of bresaola, about 150 g/5 oz total weight

50 g/2 oz wild rocket

200 g/7 oz firm ricotta cheese

olive oil, to drizzle

salt (optional) and pepper

lemon wedges, to serve

Arrange the bresaola slices on 4 plates. Scatter over the rocket and put a slice of ricotta on each plate.

Drizzle lightly with oil and season with salt if necessary (bresaola can sometimes be quite salty) and pepper.

Serve immediately with some lemon wedges on the side.

GOOD EATING

- Make the dressing. Mix together all the ingredients in a small bowl and set aside.

- Cook the sweet potatoes in lightly salted boiling water for 2 minutes. Drain well. Heat the oil in a large frying pan, add the sweet potatoes and fry for about 10 minutes, turning once, until golden.

- Meanwhile, arrange the haloumi slices on a lightly oiled, foil-lined grill rack. Cook under a preheated moderate grill for about 3 minutes until golden.

- Pile the sweet potatoes, haloumi and rocket on to serving plates and spoon over the dressing. Serve immediately.

TAKES 25 MINS
SERVES 4

500 g/1 lb sweet potatoes, sliced

3 tablespoons olive oil

250 g/8 oz haloumi cheese, patted dry on kitchen paper and thinly sliced

75 g/3 oz rocket

DRESSING

5 tablespoons olive oil

3 tablespoons clear honey

2 tablespoons lemon or lime juice

1 1/2 teaspoons black onion seeds

1 red chilli, deseeded and finely sliced

2 teaspoons chopped lemon thyme

salt and pepper

SWEET POTATO, ROCKET & HALOUMI SALAD

GREEN BEAN & TOMATO SALAD

TAKES 12 MINS
SERVES 4

250 g/8 oz mixed red and yellow baby tomatoes, plum if possible

250 g/8 oz thin green beans, trimmed

handful of chopped mint

1 garlic clove, crushed

4 tablespoons olive oil

1 tablespoon balsamic vinegar

salt and pepper

Cut the tomatoes in half and put them in a large bowl.

Cook the green beans in a saucepan of lightly salted boiling water for 3–4 minutes. Drain them thoroughly and add them to the bowl with the tomatoes.

Add the chopped mint, garlic, oil and balsamic vinegar. Season to taste with salt and pepper and mix well. Serve warm or cold.

GREEN BEANS WITH LEMON & GARLIC

TAKES 5 MINS
SERVES 4 AS A SIDE DISH

300 g/10 oz green beans

¹/₂ tablespoon olive oil

grated rind of 1 lemon

1 garlic clove, crushed

1 tablespoon roughly chopped flat leaf parsley

salt

Cook the beans in a saucepan of lightly salted boiling water for 3–4 minutes until they are just tender but still have a bite. Drain thoroughly and transfer to a bowl.

Add the remaining ingredients and season with salt. Toss to combine and serve immediately.

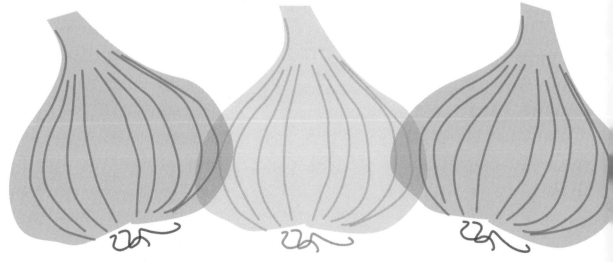

Grind the basil, pine nuts and garlic in a mortar with a pestle until the mixture forms a paste. Stir in the cheeses, then slowly add the oil, a little at a time, stirring continuously with a wooden spoon. Alternatively, blend the basil, pine nuts and garlic in a food processor or blender until the mixture forms a paste. Add the cheeses and whizz briefly, then, with the motor still running, pour in the oil through the feed tube in a thin, steady stream.

Meanwhile, cook the potatoes in a large saucepan of lightly salted boiling water for 5 minutes, then add the pasta and cook according to the instructions on the packet until it is just tender. Add the beans 5 minutes before the end of the cooking time.

Drain the pasta and vegetables, reserving 2 tablespoons of the cooking water. Return the cooked pasta and vegetables to the pan and stir in the pesto sauce, adding the reserved water to loosen the mixture. Serve immediately, scattered with some extra grated Parmesan.

TAKES 20 MINS
SERVES 4

75 g/3 oz basil leaves

25 g/1 oz pine nuts

2 garlic cloves, crushed

2 tablespoons grated Parmesan cheese, plus extra to serve

1 tablespoon grated pecorino cheese

3 tablespoons olive oil

250 g/8 oz potatoes, peeled and thinly sliced

400 g/13 oz dried linguine

150 g/5 oz green beans

PASTA ALLA GENOVESE

Cook the peas with the mint in a large saucepan of lightly salted boiling water for about 5 minutes or until very tender. Drain the peas and return them to the pan, discarding the mint.

Stir in the butter and crème fraîche and use a potato masher to crush the peas roughly. Season to taste with salt and pepper and reheat gently. Serve immediately.

**TAKES 15 MINS
SERVES 4–6**

**400 g/13 oz fresh peas,
shelled**

several sprigs of mint

25 g/1 oz butter

2 tablespoons crème fraîche

salt and pepper

CRUSHED MINTED PEAS

FRESH PEA & TOMATO FRITTATA

TAKES 20 MINS
SERVES 4

125 g/4 oz fresh peas

2 tablespoons olive oil

bunch of spring onions, sliced

1 garlic clove, crushed

125 g/4 oz cherry tomatoes, halved

6 eggs

2 tablespoons chopped mint

handful of pea shoots (optional)

rocket leaves

shavings of Parmesan cheese (optional)

salt and pepper

Cook the fresh peas in a pan of lightly salted boiling water for 3 minutes. Drain and refresh under cold water.

Heat the oil in an ovenproof, nonstick frying pan. Fry the spring onions and garlic for 2 minutes, then add the tomatoes and peas.

Beat the eggs with the mint and season with salt and pepper. Swirl the egg mixture into the pan, scatter over the pea shoots and cook over a medium heat for 3–4 minutes until almost set.

Put the pan under a preheated hot grill and cook the frittata for 2–3 minutes until lightly browned and cooked through. Leave to cool slightly and serve cut into wedges with the rocket and sprinkled with Parmesan shavings, if liked.

Cut the potatoes into chunks and cook them in a saucepan of lightly salted boiling water for about 8 minutes until softened but still retaining their firm texture.

Meanwhile, cook the peas in a separate pan of lightly salted boiling water for 2 minutes. Drain the peas, put them in a bowl and mash them with a fork until broken up. Coarsely grate the potatoes and add them to the bowl with the mint and beaten egg. Season to taste with salt and pepper and mix together until evenly combined.

Arrange alternate overlapping slices of the mozzarella and tomatoes in a shallow flameproof dish and season lightly with salt and pepper.

Make a dressing by mixing 5 tablespoons olive oil with the vinegar and basil.

Melt the butter with the remaining oil in a heavy-based frying pan. Add the potato and pea mixture and pack down gently in an even layer. Cook over a moderate heat for about 5 minutes until the underside looks crisp and golden when you lift the edge with a palette knife.

Invert the pancake on to a baking sheet or flat plate, then slide it back into the pan and fry for a further 3 minutes. While it is cooking, grill the mozzarella and tomatoes under a preheated hot grill until the mozzarella starts to melt.

Cut the pancake into wedges and transfer to serving plates. Pile the mozzarella and tomatoes on top and spoon over the dressing.

TAKES 26 MINS
SERVES 4

500 g/1 lb potatoes

250 g/8 oz peas, fresh or frozen

3 tablespoons chopped mint

1 egg, lightly beaten

300 g/10 oz mozzarella cheese, sliced

6 plum tomatoes, sliced

6 tablespoons olive oil

1 tablespoon balsamic vinegar

small handful of basil leaves, shredded

50 g/2 oz butter

salt and pepper

MINTED PEA CAKE WITH MOZZARELLA & TOMATO

MONKFISH WITH PEAS & ALMONDS

TAKES 19–21 MINS
SERVES 4

800 g/1 lb 10 oz monkfish fillet, skinned

1 onion, finely chopped

olive oil, to drizzle

15 whole blanched almonds, toasted and finely ground

3 garlic cloves, crushed

large pinch of saffron threads, crushed

1 tablespoon finely chopped flat leaf parsley

250 g/8 oz peas, fresh or frozen

salt and pepper

Cut the monkfish into 8 equal pieces. Spread the onion over the base of a medium-sized flameproof casserole and arrange the fish pieces over the top. Season to taste with salt and pepper and drizzle over a little oil. Cover tightly and cook over a medium heat for 5–6 minutes.

Meanwhile, put the ground almonds, garlic, saffron and parsley in a small bowl and blend together, adding 2–3 tablespoons water to make a smooth paste.

Spread the almond mixture over the top of the fish and add the peas. Re-cover and cook for 4–5 minutes or until the fish is cooked through. Serve immediately.

50 g/2 oz butter

500 g/1 lb cucumbers, peeled,
deseeded and cut into
1 cm/¹/₂ inch pieces

250 g/8 oz peas, fresh or frozen

pinch of caster sugar

¹/₄ teaspoon white pepper

3 tablespoons finely chopped
mint

1.2 litres/2 pints vegetable stock

175 g/6 oz potatoes, chopped

150 ml/¹/₄ pint double cream

salt

Heat the butter in a large, heavy-based saucepan. Add the cucumber and cook over a moderate heat for 5 minutes, then add the peas, sugar, white pepper and 2 tablespoons of the mint.

Pour in the stock and bring to the boil. Add the potatoes, reduce the heat, partially cover and simmer for 20 minutes or until the potatoes are tender.

Put the soup in a food processor or blender and whizz, in batches if necessary, until smooth, then transfer it to a clean saucepan or, if it is to be served cold, to a bowl. Season to taste with salt.

If the soup is to be served hot add the cream and reheat gently without boiling. Serve in warm soup bowls, garnishing each portion with a little of the remaining mint.

If the soup is to be served cold cover the bowl closely and chill for at least 3 hours, making sure that the cream is also chilled. Just before serving, fold the chilled cream into the soup. Serve in chilled bowls, garnishing each portion with some of the remaining mint.

MINT, CUCUMBER & GREEN PEA SOUP

BROAD BEANS WITH HAM

TAKES 1½ HRS
SERVES 4

800 g / 1 lb 10 oz fresh broad beans in their pods

2–3 tablespoons olive oil

2 garlic cloves, thinly sliced

1 small onion, finely chopped

4 tablespoons finely chopped Serrano ham

200 ml/7 fl oz fino sherry

200 ml/7 fl oz water

1 teaspoon finely chopped marjoram leaves

2 hard-boiled eggs, shelled and finely chopped

salt and pepper

Remove the beans from their pods. Heat the oil in a large, heavy-based saucepan. Add the garlic, onion and ham and cook, stirring, for 3–4 minutes. Add the beans, sherry, measured water and marjoram, season to taste with salt and pepper and bring to the boil. Reduce the heat to low, cover the pan and simmer gently for 1 hour or until the beans are tender.

Uncover the pan and cook until the remaining liquid has evaporated (the mixture should be moist, but not too liquid).

Transfer the mixture to a warm serving dish and scatter over the eggs. Serve immediately.

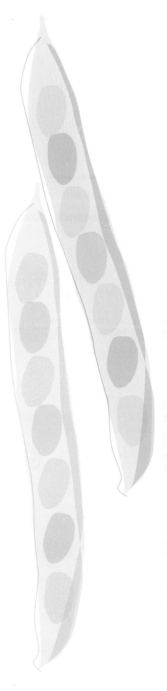

BROAD BEAN, PROSCIUTTO & MINT PASTA SAUCE

TAKES 18–20 MINS
SERVES 4

350 g/11½ oz fusilli

250 g/8 oz baby broad beans, shelled

4–6 tablespoons olive oil

rind of 1 lemon

175 g/6 oz prosciutto, shredded

3–4 spring onions, finely sliced

8–10 mint leaves, shredded

125 g/4 oz buffalo mozzarella, diced

salt

Cook the pasta in a large saucepan of lightly salted boiling water for 10–12 minutes or according to the instructions on the packet. Drain well.

Meanwhile, bring a pan of salted water to the boil and cook the broad beans for 2–3 minutes. Drain the beans quickly and toss them in the oil with the lemon rind, prosciutto, spring onions and mint leaves.

Toss the freshly cooked pasta with the sauce, then tip on to warm serving dishes. Scatter over the mozzarella and serve immediately.

I thin French baguette

olive oil, for brushing and mixing

250 g/8 oz fresh broad beans, shelled

I small ripe pear, peeled, cored and finely chopped

drop of balsamic or sherry vinegar

125 g/4 oz pecorino, salted ricotta or feta cheese, cut into small dice

salt and pepper

Cut the bread into thin rounds, brush them with olive oil and arrange the slices on a baking sheet. Cook in a preheated oven, 190°C/375°F, Gas Mark 5, for about 10 minutes or until golden and crisp.

Meanwhile, blanch the beans for 3 minutes in a saucepan of lightly salted boiling water. Drain and refresh in cold water. Pop the beans out of their skins and mash them roughly using a fork. Add a little olive oil to moisten the beans and season well with salt and pepper.

Mix the chopped pear with a drop of balsamic or sherry vinegar, add the cheese and stir to mix.

Spread each crostini with a mound of bean purée and top with a spoonful of the pear and cheese mixture. Serve immediately.

BROAD BEAN, PEAR & PECORINO CROSTINI

Score the skin of each duck portion several times with a sharp knife. Season the flour and use it to coat the duck legs. Heat the oil in a large, heavy-based frying pan. Fry the duck, in batches, until deep golden then transfer to a roasting tin.

Drain all but 1 tablespoon of the oil from the pan and fry the onions and garlic for 3 minutes. Blend in the wine, stock, bay leaves and a little salt and pepper and bring to the boil. Pour the liquid over the duck, cover and cook in a preheated oven, 160° C/325°F/Gas Mark 3, for 45 minutes.

Stir in the mint, broad beans and carrots. Cover and return to the oven for a further 30–40 minutes until tender.

Drain and transfer the duck to warm serving plates. Stir the cream into juices in the roasting tin and let it bubble on the hob for 2 minutes. Pour the sauce around the duck before serving.

TAKES 2 HRS
SERVES 6

6 large duck legs, each about 300 g/12 oz, halved

1 tablespoon plain flour

2 tablespoons olive oil

2 onions, sliced

2 garlic cloves, sliced

125 ml/4 fl oz white wine

600 ml/1 pint duck or chicken stock

3 bay leaves

4 tablespoons chopped mint

175 g/6 oz baby broad beans

200 g/7 oz baby carrots

100 ml/3½ fl oz double cream

salt and pepper

BRAISED MINTED DUCK WITH BROAD BEANS

PENNE WITH BROAD BEANS & ARTICHOKE PESTO

TAKES 22 MINS
SERVES 4

375 g/12 oz dried penne

375 g/12 oz frozen broad beans

75 g/3 oz marinated charred artichokes, roughly chopped

1 garlic clove, chopped

15 g/½ oz parsley, chopped

1 tablespoon pine nuts

15 g/½ oz pecorino cheese, grated, plus extra to serve

150 ml/¼ pint olive oil

salt and pepper

Cook the pasta in a large saucepan of lightly salted boiling water for 10–12 minutes or according to the instructions on the packet until just tender. At the same time, blanch the broad beans in a pan of lightly salted boiling water for 3 minutes. Drain and set aside.

Put the artichokes, garlic, parsley and pine nuts in a food processor and whizz to make a fairly smooth paste. Transfer the mixture to a bowl and stir in the pecorino and oil. Season to taste with salt and pepper.

Drain the pasta, reserving 4 tablespoons of the cooking liquid, and return it to the pan. Add the pesto mixture, broad beans and reserved cooking liquid and season to taste with pepper. Toss over a medium heat until warmed through. Serve with extra grated cheese.

TOMATOES

WE HAVE COME TO TAKE TOMATOES FOR GRANTED. THEY ARE ON THE SUPERMARKET SHELVES ALL YEAR ROUND BUT ARE OFTEN FLAVOURLESS AND HAVE LITTLE TEXTURE. ANYONE WHO HAS GROWN THEIR OWN KNOWS THAT HOME-GROWN TOMATOES HAVE A FLAVOUR THAT IS UNSURPASSED. WELL-GROWN AND WELL-RIPENED TOMATOES TRULY ARE A TASTE OF SUMMER. MOREOVER, THEY ARE EASY TO GROW AND WITH JUST A LITTLE CARE WILL REWARD YOU WITH AN ABUNDANCE OF FRUIT FOR MONTHS ON END.

IT IS THOUGHT THAT THE TOMATO CAME FROM PERU, WHERE IT THRIVED IN THE WARM, DAMP CONDITIONS. THE PERUVIANS DID NOT RECOGNIZE THIS PLANT'S CULINARY POTENTIAL, AND IT WASN'T UNTIL THE 4TH CENTURY AD THAT IT BECAME PART OF A FOOD CROP IN MEXICO, FROM WHERE IT TRAVELLED TO EUROPE, GAINING POPULARITY EVERYWHERE IT WENT.

GOOD FOR YOU

Not only do tomatoes look and taste great, but they are also good for you. They are packed with vitamins A, C and E and have no fat or cholesterol, and each fruit has only about 15 calories. However, it is the colour that is the key to all the benefits they have to offer. The natural red pigment in tomatoes, called lycopene, is an antioxidant that is thought to prevent cancer and many other serious diseases. Home-grown tomatoes have a much higher content of lycopene than their imported, long-life cousins, so there is even more reason to grow your own. Some of the nutrients can be lost in the cooking process, but there are so many ways to make the best of tomatoes without cooking them that there is no excuse for not eating more.

FIVE OF THE BEST

Gardener's Delight This popular cultivar is a sweet cherry tomato, reliably bearing an abundance of fruits.
Sungold The orange-red, exceptionally sweet cherry tomatoes are an ideal choice for salads and salsas. The vine will need some protection from cold winds.

Tornado This is a hardy cultivar and reliable cropper, producing plenty of early-ripening and tasty, small red fruits.
Alicante A reliable cultivar, this bears fruits with a smooth, red skin and a good flavour.
Golden Sunrise The medium-sized tomatoes have a rich yellow skin and a unique fruity taste.

DELICIOUS IDEAS TO TRY

Salsa Remove the seeds from 6 tomatoes and chop the flesh up with a red onion, a handful of chopped fresh coriander and a dash of red wine vinegar. Mix together and serve with grilled fish or steak.
Salad Mix cool, steamed green beans with cherry tomatoes, add a good dash of balsamic vinegar and serve with fish, chicken or pork.
Roast Sprinkle 6 vine tomatoes with sugar and roast in a hot oven. Serve with lamb and green vegetables.

Sauce Roast 500 g/1 lb cherry tomatoes with some chopped garlic, a sprinkling of fennel seeds and a dash of olive oil. Stir into cooked pasta and serve with a green salad.
Soup Add 1 kg/2 lb skinned, chopped tomatoes to a large pan with some olive oil, a chopped onion and a couple of chopped garlic cloves, allow to soften, then simmer for 30 minutes with 600 ml/1 pint vegetable stock. Add a couple of handfuls of basil leaves and season to taste.

TOP TIPS FOR TOMATOES

Store tomatoes at room temperature to make sure they retain their flavour.

Over-ripe tomatoes are great for making sauces. Green tomatoes are perfect for chutney (see page 108).

To remove the skin score a cross in the end of each fruit and immerse it in boiling water for about 15 seconds. The skin should peel away easily.

FRESH TOMATO & ALMOND SOUP

TAKES 35 MINS
SERVES 4

1 kg/2 lb vine-ripened tomatoes, roughly chopped

2 garlic cloves, crushed

300 ml/¹/₂ pint vegetable stock

2 tablespoons olive oil

1 teaspoon caster sugar

100 g/3¹/₂ oz ground toasted almonds

salt and pepper

BASIL OIL

150 ml/¹/₄ pint olive oil

15 g/¹/₂ oz basil leaves

Put the tomatoes in a large, heavy-based saucepan with the garlic, stock, oil and sugar. Season to taste with salt and pepper. Bring to the boil, then reduce the heat and simmer gently for 15 minutes.

Meanwhile, make the basil oil. Blend the oil and basil leaves in a food processor or blender with a pinch of salt until really smooth. Set aside.

Stir the ground almonds into the soup, heat through and then serve in warm soup bowls, drizzled with the basil oil.

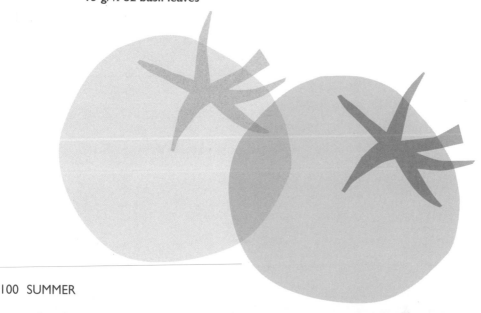

TAKES 30 MINS, PLUS STANDING
SERVES 4

4 slices of ciabatta bread

4 ripe tomatoes

$\frac{1}{2}$ cucumber, peeled

I red onion

handful of chopped flat leaf parsley

I tablespoon chopped black pitted olives

4 tablespoons olive oil

I–2 tablespoons wine vinegar

2 tablespoons lemon juice

salt and pepper

Cut or tear the bread into small pieces and put them in a large bowl.

Remove the green core from the tomatoes. Chop the flesh and add to the bread.

Cut the cucumber into quarters lengthways and then into dice. Add the cucumber to the bread and tomatoes. Chop the onion and add to the bowl with the parsley and olives.

Mix together the olive oil, vinegar and lemon juice and season to taste with salt and pepper. Pour the dressing over the salad and mix well. Cover and leave to stand at room temperature for at least I hour before serving, to allow all the flavours to steep and mingle.

PANZANELLA

TAKES 25–30 MINS
SERVES 4

75 g/3 oz instant polenta or
cornmeal

500 ml/17 fl oz simmering water

75 g/3 oz butter

40 g/1½ oz Parmesan cheese,
grated

6 tablespoons chopped herbs,
such as chervil, chives and
parsley

salt and pepper

SPICY TOMATO SALSA

300 g/10 oz ripe cherry
tomatoes, quartered

2 fresh red chillies, deseeded and
finely chopped

1 small red onion, finely chopped

2 tablespoons chilli oil

2 tablespoons olive oil

2 tablespoons lime juice

2 tablespoons shredded mint

Pour the polenta into a pan of the simmering measured water and beat with a wooden spoon until it is thick and smooth. Reduce the heat and continue stirring for about 5 minutes or according to the instructions on the packet until cooked. Remove the pan from the heat, add the butter, Parmesan and herbs and stir to combine. Season to taste with salt and pepper, then turn the polenta into a greased 25 cm/10 inch cake tin, at least 2.5 cm/1 inch deep. Smooth the top with the back of a spoon and leave to set for 5–10 minutes.

Meanwhile, combine all the salsa ingredients in a bowl and season with salt and pepper to taste. Set aside.

Remove the set polenta from the tin and cut it into 8 wedges. Heat a griddle pan, put the wedges on the griddle and cook for 2–3 minutes on each side until heated through and golden. Serve with the salsa.

HERBY POLENTA WEDGES WITH SPICY TOMATO SALSA

CHERRY TOMATO TARTS WITH PESTO CREAM

TAKES 28 MINS
SERVES 4

2 tablespoons olive oil

1 onion, finely chopped

375 g/12 oz cherry tomatoes

2 garlic cloves, crushed

3 tablespoons sun-dried tomato paste

325 g/11 oz puff pastry, thawed if frozen

beaten egg, to glaze

150 ml/5 fl oz crème fraîche

2 tablespoons pesto

salt and pepper

basil leaves, to garnish

Lightly grease a large baking sheet and sprinkle with water. Heat the oil in a frying pan. Add the onion and fry for about 3 minutes until softened. Halve about 150 g/5 oz of the tomatoes. Remove the pan from the heat, add the garlic and sun-dried tomato paste, then stir in all the tomatoes, turning them until they are lightly coated in the sauce.

Roll out the pastry on a lightly floured surface and cut out 4 rounds, each 12 cm/5 inches across, using a cutter or small bowl as a guide. Transfer to the prepared baking sheet and use the tip of a sharp knife to make a shallow cut 1 cm/½ inch in from the edge of each round to form a rim. Brush the rims with beaten egg.

Pile the tomato mixture on to the centres of the pastries, making sure the mixture stays within the rims.

Cook the tarts in a preheated oven, 220°C /425°F/Gas Mark 7, for about 15 minutes until the pastry is risen and golden.

Meanwhile, lightly mix together the crème fraîche, pesto and salt and pepper in a bowl so that the crème fraîche is streaked with the pesto.

When the tarts are cooked transfer them to serving plates and spoon over the crème fraîche and pesto mixture. Garnish with basil leaves and serve immediately.

STUFFED TOMATOES

TAKES 27–35 MINS
SERVES 4

4 large ripe tomatoes

2 tablespoons olive oil

2 tablespoons pine nuts

3 garlic cloves, finely chopped

100 g/3^1/$_2$ oz fresh white breadcrumbs

1 tablespoon chopped tarragon leaves

1 tablespoon chopped flat leaf parsley

salt and pepper

Cut the tomatoes in half widthways and scoop out and discard the seeds. Use a small teaspoon to hollow out the tomato shells, reserving the flesh. Arrange the tomato halves, cut side up, on a baking sheet.

Heat the oil in a nonstick frying pan, add the pine nuts and cook over a medium heat, stirring, for 2–3 minutes. Add the garlic, breadcrumbs and herbs and cook, stirring, for 3–4 minutes. Add the reserved tomato flesh, season to taste with salt and pepper and cook, continuing to stir, for 2–3 minutes.

Spoon an equal quantity of the mixture into each tomato shell and bake in a preheated oven, 180°C /350°F/Gas Mark 4, for 15–20 minutes until the tomatoes have softened.

Remove the tomatoes from the oven and leave to cool to room temperature before serving.

TAKES 35 MINS
SERVES 4

250 g/8 oz linguine

plenty of grated Parmesan cheese

salt

TOMATO SAUCE

12 tomatoes

4 tablespoons olive oil

2 small onions, finely chopped

3 tablespoons sun-dried tomato paste

3 garlic cloves, crushed or finely chopped

1 teaspoon caster sugar

about 12 large leaves of basil

Make the tomato sauce. Put the tomatoes in a heatproof bowl and just cover with the freshly boiled water. Leave to stand for 1–2 minutes or until the tomato skins start to split. Carefully pour off the hot water and peel away the tomato skins. (Make sure they have cooled down before you pick them up.) Roughly chop the tomatoes.

Heat 3 tablespoons oil in a large saucepan and gently fry the onions for 5 minutes. Add the chopped tomatoes, tomato paste, garlic and sugar. Cover and cook over a gentle heat for 15 minutes, stirring the sauce occasionally until it is thick and pulpy.

Meanwhile, cook the linguine in lightly salted boiling water for about 10 minutes or according to the instructions on the packet until it is just tender, stirring frequently to break up any bits of pasta that are sticking together. Drain thoroughly, reserving a small amount of the liquid, and return to the pan

Add the reserved water to the saucepan and stir in the remaining oil. Tear the basil leaves into the tomato sauce.

Pile mounds of the linguine into individual warm serving dishes and spoon the sauce on top. Serve immediately with plenty of Parmesan cheese.

LINGUINE WITH TOMATO SAUCE

HERBY PENNE WITH CHERRY TOMATOES

TAKES 25 MINS
SERVES 4

375 g/12 oz dried penne

200 g/7 oz cherry tomatoes, halved

2 tablespoons pesto

1 tablespoon white wine vinegar

2 tablespoons capers, drained

2 tablespoons chopped mixed herbs, such as parsley and basil

salt and pepper

Parmesan cheese shavings, to serve

Cook the penne in a large saucepan of lightly salted boiling water for 10–12 minutes or according to the instructions on the packet until it is just tender. Drain thoroughly.

Meanwhile, cook the tomatoes under a preheated hot grill for about 15 minutes until they are slightly charred and beginning to look dry.

Transfer the pesto, vinegar, capers and herbs to a food processor or blender and whizz until the mixture is almost smooth but still retains a little texture.

Toss the sauce through the pasta with the tomatoes and season to taste with salt and pepper. Serve immediately, scattered with Parmesan shavings.

CHORIZO-STUFFED PLAICE WITH TOMATOES

TAKES 45 MINS
SERVES 4

100 g/3½ oz chorizo sausage

50 g/2 oz fresh breadcrumbs

2 tablespoons sun-dried tomato paste

5 tablespoons olive oil

8 skinned fillets from 2 large plaice

8 small ripe tomatoes or 4 large tomatoes, halved

several sprigs of thyme

splash of white wine

salt and pepper

Cut the chorizo into pieces and whizz in a food processor until it is finely chopped. Add the breadcrumbs, tomato paste and 1 tablespoon of the oil and whizz until combined.

Lay the fish fillets, skinned side up, on your work surface. Spread each with a thin layer of the chorizo mixture and roll them up, starting from the thick end.

Put the fish rolls in a large, shallow, ovenproof dish and tuck the tomatoes and thyme around them. Drizzle with the remaining oil and the wine and season lightly with salt and pepper.

Bake the fish in a preheated oven, 200°C/400°F/Gas Mark 6, for 20–25 minutes or until cooked through. Serve immediately.

GREEN TOMATO CHUTNEY

TAKES 1³/₄–2 HRS
MAKES ABOUT 2 KG/4 LB

1 kg/2 lb green tomatoes, finely chopped

500 g/1 lb onions, finely chopped

500 g/1 lb cooking apples, peeled, cored and chopped

2 fresh green chillies, halved, deseeded and finely chopped

2 garlic cloves, crushed

1 teaspoon ground ginger

generous pinch of ground cloves

generous pinch of ground turmeric

50 g/2 oz raisins

250 g/8 oz soft dark brown sugar

300 ml/¹/₂ pint white wine vinegar

Put the tomatoes, onions, apples and chillies into a large saucepan and mix together. Add the garlic, ginger, cloves and turmeric, then stir in the raisins, sugar and vinegar.

Bring the mixture to the boil, reduce the heat and cover the pan. Simmer, stirring frequently, for 1¹/₄–1¹/₂ hours or until the chutney has thickened.

Transfer the chutney to warm, dry jars. Cover the surface of each one with a disc of waxed paper, waxed side down, then top with an airtight lid. Label and leave to mature in a cool, dark place for at least 3 weeks before using, or store, unopened, for 6–12 months.

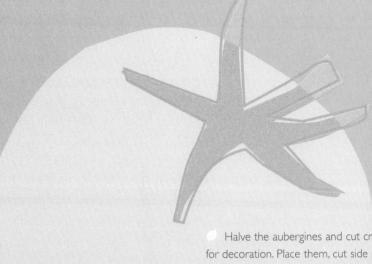

Halve the aubergines and cut criss-cross lines over the cut surfaces for decoration. Place them, cut side up, on a foil-lined grill rack and drizzle with 1 tablespoon of the oil, the lemon juice and salt and pepper. Grill under a preheated hot grill for 8–10 minutes, turning once, until the slices are tender and golden. Sprinkle over the chervil or parsley.

Meanwhile, put the tomatoes in a frying pan with another tablespoon of the oil and sprinkle with the sugar, garlic and salt and pepper. Fry quickly for 1–2 minutes until they are softened but not mushy.

Arrange the aubergines on warm serving plates, pile the ricotta, then the tomatoes and finally the rocket on top.

Add the balsamic vinegar, the remaining oil, salt and pepper and any juices on the foil to the frying pan and heat through, stirring, for 30 seconds. Pour over the salad before serving.

GRILLED BABY AUBERGINE & TOMATO SALAD

Heat the oil in a large frying pan. Fry the aubergines and onions for 8–10 minutes until golden and tender. Add the pine nuts and garlic and fry for 2 minutes. Stir in the tomato paste and stock and cook for 2 minutes.

Meanwhile, cook the pasta in lightly salted boiling water for about 2 minutes or according to the instructions on the packet until just tender.

Drain the pasta and return it to the pan. Add the sauce and olives, season to taste with salt and pepper and toss together over a moderate heat for 1 minute until combined. Scatter over the parsley and serve immediately.

TAKES 22 MINS
SERVES 4

8 tablespoons olive oil

2 aubergines, diced

2 red onions, sliced

75 g/3 oz pine nuts

3 garlic cloves, crushed

5 tablespoons sun-dried tomato paste

150 ml/¹/₄ pint vegetable stock

300 g/10 oz cracked pepper, tomato or mushroom-flavoured fresh ribbon pasta

100 g/3¹/₂ oz pitted black olives

salt and pepper

3 tablespoons roughly chopped flat leaf parsley, to garnish

RIBBON PASTA WITH AUBERGINES & PINE NUTS

GROW IT, CO

STUFFED AUBERGINES

TAKES 30 MINS
SERVES 4

2 aubergines

4 tablespoons olive oil

8 tomatoes, skinned and chopped

2 garlic cloves, crushed or chopped

4 anchovy fillets, chopped

1 tablespoon capers, chopped

handful of basil, chopped

handful of flat leaf parsley, chopped

75 g/3 oz pecorino cheese, grated

2 tablespoons pine nuts, toasted

50 g/2 oz white breadcrumbs

salt and pepper

Cut the aubergines in half lengthways and scoop out the flesh, taking care not to break the skin. Roughly chop the flesh.

Heat the oil in a large frying pan. Add the aubergine shells and cook them on each side for 3–4 minutes and transfer them to a lightly oiled baking dish. Add the aubergine flesh to the frying pan and cook until golden brown.

Mix together in a bowl the chopped tomatoes, garlic, anchovies, capers, basil, parsley, half the pecorino, the pine nuts, breadcrumbs and aubergine flesh. Season to taste with salt and pepper.

Spoon the mixture into the sautéed aubergine shells, piling it high. Sprinkle over the remaining pecorino and cook in a preheated oven, 200°C/400°F/Gas Mark 6, for 20 minutes. Serve immediately.

OK IT, EAT IT

Heat 1 of the tablespoons of oil in a heavy-based saucepan. Fry the onion and garlic for 3 minutes.

Add the tomatoes and chilli and cook gently for about 8–10 minutes until the sauce has reduced. Add the basil and season well with salt and pepper.

Heat the remaining olive oil in a large frying pan, add the aubergine slices and fry until golden on each side.

Place a layer of aubergines in a shallow, ovenproof dish and spoon over half of the sauce. Add another layer of aubergine slices, then add the rest of the sauce and finally crumble over the Gorgonzola. Bake in a preheated oven, 190°C/375°F/Gas Mark 5, for 15 minutes. Serve immediately.

BAKED AUBERGINE & GORGONZOLA

TAKES 30 MINS
SERVES 4

4 tablespoons olive oil

1 red onion, chopped

2 garlic cloves, crushed and chopped

400 g/13 oz can chopped tomatoes

1 red chilli, diced

handful of basil, roughly torn

2 aubergines, thickly sliced

125 g/4 oz Gorgonzola cheese

salt and pepper

ROASTED AUBERGINE SOUP

TAKES 50–55 MINS
SERVES 4

2–3 large aubergines, about 1 kg/2 lb in total

3 tablespoons olive oil

1 red onion

2 garlic cloves, crushed

1.2 litres/2 pints chicken stock

salt and pepper

MINTY YOGURT

200 ml/7 fl oz crème fraîche or Greek yogurt

2 tablespoons chopped mint

Put the aubergines under a preheated hot grill and cook, turning occasionally, for 20 minutes or until the skin is well charred and the flesh has softened. Leave to cool slightly. Cut the aubergines in half and scoop out and chop the flesh.

Heat the oil in a large, heavy-based saucepan. Add the onion and garlic and cook over a moderate heat for 5 minutes or until softened. Add the chopped aubergine and the stock and cook for 10–15 minutes.

Put the soup in a food processor or blender and whizz, in batches if necessary, until smooth. Strain through a sieve into the saucepan. Reheat gently and season to taste with salt and pepper.

Make the minty yogart. Mix the crème fraîche or yogurt with the mint and season to taste with salt and pepper.

Serve the soup in warm soup bowls, garnished with a spoonful of the minted crème fraîche or yogurt.

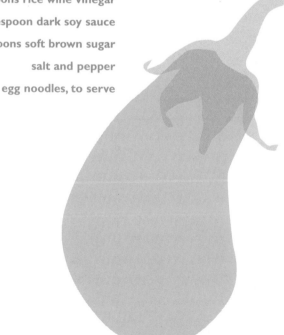

Heat the oil in a wok or large frying pan. Add the aubergine and cook for 5 minutes, stirring frequently so that it cooks evenly. Add the garlic and ginger and stir-fry for 2 minutes.

Mix together half the spring onions with the remaining ingredients and add to the wok or frying pan. Stir thoroughly, season to taste with salt and pepper then scatter over the remaining spring onions.

Serve immediately with egg noodles.

SZECHUAN AUBERGINE

TAKES 22 MINS
SERVES 4

5 tablespoons vegetable oil

1 large aubergine, cut into 2.5 cm/1 inch cubes

2 large garlic cloves, crushed

1 tablespoon grated fresh root ginger

6 spring onions, sliced

2 tablespoons chilli sauce

2 tablespoons yellow bean sauce

2 tablespoons dry sherry

2 tablespoons rice wine vinegar

1 tablespoon dark soy sauce

2 tablespoons soft brown sugar

salt and pepper

egg noodles, to serve

GRIDDLED POTATOES WITH WASABI SAUCE

TAKES 50 MINS, PLUS STANDING
SERVES 4

750 g/1 ¹/₂ lb new potatoes

5 tablespoons mayonnaise

3 tablespoons water

wasabi paste, to taste

salt

Heat a griddle pan. Cut the potatoes in half lengthways, put a batch on the griddle and cook for 10 minutes on each side. When they are almost soft, remove them from the griddle, transfer them into a dish and leave to stand for 10 minutes to steam in their skins. Sprinkle with a little salt. Repeat with the remaining potatoes.

Blend the mayonnaise, measured water and a little wasabi paste in a small bowl.

Serve the potatoes with the wasabi-flavoured mayonnaise.

CAJUN POTATO, PRAWN & AVOCADO SALAD

TAKES 25–30 MINS
SERVES 2

300 g/10 oz baby new potatoes

1 tablespoon olive oil

250 g/8 oz cooked peeled king prawns

1 garlic clove, crushed

4 spring onions, finely sliced

2 teaspoons Cajun seasoning

1 ripe avocado, stoned, peeled and diced

handful of alfalfa sprouts

salt

Cut the potatoes in half and cook them in a large saucepan of lightly salted boiling water for 10–15 minutes or until tender. Drain well.

Heat the oil in a large, nonstick frying pan and stir-fry the prawns, garlic, spring onions and Cajun seasoning for 2–3 minutes or until the prawns are hot. Add in the potatoes and cook for a further 1 minute. Transfer to a warm serving dish.

Stir in the avocado, top with the alfalfa sprouts and serve while still warm.

6 tablespoons olive oil, plus extra
to serve

2 teaspoons chopped thyme

grated rind of 1 lemon

4 tuna steaks, each about
200 g/7 oz

750 g/1½ lb new potatoes,
scrubbed

2 garlic cloves, crushed

50 g/2 oz watercress leaves

salt and pepper

🍃 Mix 2 tablespoons of the oil with the thyme and lemon rind and season with salt and pepper. Rub the mixture all over the tuna and leave to marinate until required.

🍃 Cook the potatoes in a saucepan of lightly salted boiling water for 12–15 minutes or until just tender.

🍃 Heat the remaining oil in a small frying pan and fry the garlic for 3–4 minutes until soft but not golden.

🍃 Drain the potatoes, return them to the pan and use a potato masher to lightly crush them with the garlic oil. Season with salt and pepper and keep them warm.

🍃 Cook the tuna steaks in a preheated ridged grill pan for about 45 seconds on each side. Wrap the fish in foil and leave to rest for 5 minutes.

🍃 Stir the watercress into the potatoes until the leaves have wilted slightly, spoon on to plates and serve topped with the tuna.

TUNA WITH CRUSHED POTATOES & WATERCRESS

12 new potatoes, cooked and unpeeled

12 long, thin slices of prosciutto

sea salt flakes and pepper

🌿 Wrap each of the potatoes in a slice of the prosciutto.

🌿 Heat a griddle pan, add the wrapped potatoes and cook, for about 8 minutes, on all sides until the prosciutto is golden and crunchy.

🌿 Serve sprinkled with sea salt and pepper.

NEW POTATOES WITH PROSCIUTTO

DIG FOR YO

JERSEY ROYAL POTATOES & CELERY SALAD

TAKES 27 MINS
SERVES 4–6

500 g/1 lb small Jersey Royal potatoes, scrubbed

6 celery sticks, with leaves if possible

75 g/3 oz black olives

3 tablespoons capers, rinsed and drained

few sprigs of parsley, roughly chopped

salt and pepper

TARRAGON AND LEMON DRESSING

2 tablespoons tarragon vinegar

1 teaspoon finely grated lemon rind

1/4 teaspoon Dijon mustard

1 tablespoon chopped tarragon

pinch of sugar

5 tablespoons olive oil or grapeseed oil

salt and pepper

Make the dressing. Combine the vinegar, lemon rind, mustard and tarragon in a small bowl then season to taste with salt and pepper and add a pinch of sugar. Stir to mix, then gradually whisk in the oil using a balloon whisk.

Cook the potatoes in a saucepan of lightly salted boiling water for about 12 minutes or until just tender. Drain and refresh under cold running water. Drain thoroughly and leave to cool.

Slice the celery sticks diagonally and roughly chop any leaves. Put them in a bowl with the olives, capers and parsley. Add the cooled potatoes and season with salt and pepper.

Pour the dressing over the salad, toss well and serve.

UR DINNER

TAKES 50 MINS
SERVES 4

375 g/12 oz skinless tuna

8 small potatoes, cooked and sliced

6 tomatoes, skinned and quartered

250 g/8 oz cooked green beans

1 red onion, sliced

1 cos lettuce heart, cut into quarters

4 anchovy fillets, cut lengthways

4 hard-boiled eggs, sliced or quartered

8 black olives

1 tablespoon chopped flat-leaf parsley

DRESSING

1 tablespoon wine vinegar

4 tablespoons lemon juice

4 tablespoons olive oil

1 garlic clove, crushed and chopped

1 teaspoon mustard

sea salt flakes and pepper

Heat a griddle pan and cook the tuna for 2 minutes on each side if you like it rare or for 4 minutes on each side if you prefer it well done. Remove and allow to rest for 5 minutes.

Meanwhile, make the dressing. Whizz all the ingredients in a blender or put them in a small bowl and combine with a ballon whisk. Transfer to a bowl and set aside.

Mix together the potatoes, tomatoes, green beans, onion and lettuce in a large salad bowl. Arrange the anchovy fillets, hard-boiled eggs and olives on top.

Slice the tuna and arrange the slices around the salad mixture. Spoon the dressing over the salad, garnish with chopped parsley and serve.

TUNA SALAD NIÇOISE

AROMATIC DRESSED ARTICHOKES

TAKES 40–45 MINS, PLUS
STANDING
SERVES 4 AS A TAPA

4 globe artichokes

2 tablespoons lemon juice

2 garlic cloves, crushed

I teaspoon ground cumin

I teaspoon ground coriander

$^1/_2$ teaspoon dried red chilli flakes

I tablespoon finely chopped oregano leaves

2 tablespoons sherry vinegar

2 tablespoons vegetable stock

4 tablespoons olive oil

salt and pepper

finely chopped flat leaf parsley, to garnish

Trim the artichokes, cutting off the stalks to within 5 cm/2 inches of the base, and remove and discard the tough outer leaves. Cut off the top quarter of the leaves from each artichoke and cut the artichokes lengthways in half or in quarters if large.

Use a teaspoon to scoop out and discard the hairy choke from the centre of the artichoke sections. Put them in a bowl of water adding the lemon juice to prevent discoloration.

Bring a large saucepan of lightly salted water to the boil, add the artichokes and return to the boil. Reduce the heat and simmer gently for 20–25 minutes or until tender. Remove them with a slotted spoon, drain, and put them, cut side down, on kitchen paper and leave to cool.

Meanwhile, make the dressing. Mix together the garlic, cumin, coriander, chilli flakes, oregano, vinegar, stock and oil in a bowl until well combined. Season to taste with salt and pepper.

Arrange the artichokes in a shallow serving dish in a single layer. Pour over the dressing, cover and leave to stand at room temperature for 15–20 minutes before serving, garnished with chopped parsley.

TAKES 40–45 MINS
SERVES 4

12 baby artichokes

2 tablespoons lemon juice

2 tablespoons finely chopped parsley

2 tablespoons finely chopped mint

2 garlic cloves, crushed

2 tablespoons olive oil

salt and pepper

Pull off the tough outer leaves of the artichoke, exposing the paler tender leaves, then cut about 2.5 cm/1 inch off the top. Trim the stalks, leaving about 3.5 cm/1½ inches, then peel with a potato peeler to reveal the lighter core. Baby artichokes have an edible tender choke, but if you are using larger ones, open the central leaves and scoop out and discard the hairy choke with a teaspoon. As you prepare them, place the artichokes in a bowl of cold water with the lemon juice to prevent discoloration.

Combine the parsley, mint and garlic and season with salt. Drain the artichokes and place a large pinch of the herb mixture in the central cavity of each one. Stand the artichokes, stuffed side down, in a heavy-based saucepan in which they fit snugly in a single layer. Pour in enough water to come a quarter of the way up the artichokes, then drizzle with the oil and scatter over the remaining herb mixture. Season with salt and pepper.

Bring the water to the boil over a high heat, then reduce the heat to a gentle simmer. Cover the pan with greaseproof paper, to help retain a steamy atmosphere close to the artichokes, and a tight-fitting lid. Cook the artichokes for 20–25 minutes or until tender when pierced with a fork. Leave them to cool before serving. They are best eaten just warm or at room temperature.

BRAISED ARTICHOKES WITH MINT

GRILLED SUMMER VEGETABLE & SAUSAGE PIE

TAKES 1 HR 35 MINS–1 HR 50 MINS
SERVES 8

1 red and 1 yellow pepper, quartered and deseeded

500 g/1 lb Cumberland or Lincolnshire sausages, skinned

handful of basil leaves, roughly chopped

1 aubergine, sliced

bunch of spring onions, roughly chopped

250 g/8 oz haloumi cheese, sliced

375 g/12 oz courgettes, sliced lengthways

salt and pepper

PASTRY

375 g/12 oz plain flour

175 ml/6 fl oz water

75 g/3 oz butter

beaten egg to glaze

Lightly butter a 20 cm/8 inch springform tin. Grill the peppers, skin side up, under a hot grill until the skin is charred. When they are cool enough to handle, peel away the skins.

Make the pastry. Put the flour in a mixing bowl and season with salt and pepper. Put the measured water in a saucepan, add the butter and bring to a simmer. Make a well in the centre of the flour, pour in the hot liquid and mix with a fork to form a hot dough. Knead briefly, then wrap in clingfilm. Leave to rest on the worktop for 15 minutes.

Roll out two-thirds of the dough on a lightly floured surface and carefully line the tin, pinching together any cracks. Press the sausage meat in the base of the pastry case, then add layers of the peppers, basil, aubergine, spring onions, haloumi and courgettes, seasoning with salt and pepper between layers.

Brush the edge of the pastry with a little beaten egg, then roll out the remaining pastry and cover the pie. Pinch the edges to seal, then pinch the edges all round to decorate. Make a hole in the centre of the pie to allow the steam to escape, then brush the top with egg.

Bake the pie in a preheated oven, 190°C/375°F/Gas 5, for 1–1¼ hours until the pastry is a rich golden brown. Leave to cool in the tin for 15 minutes, then remove and leave to cool if serving cold. Serve the pie warm or cold cut into slices.

THAI VEGETABLE CURRY

TAKES *30 MINS*
SERVES 2

2 teaspoons groundnut or vegetable oil

2 small onions, sliced

2 small green peppers, cored, deseeded
and chopped

2 small red peppers, cored, deseeded
and chopped

6 baby aubergines, halved, or
250 g/8 oz large aubergine, chopped

6 baby courgettes, halved lengthways,
or 2 medium courgettes, chopped

175 g/6 oz shiitake mushrooms

2 teaspoons green Thai curry paste

300 ml/¹/₂ pint coconut milk

200 ml/7 fl oz vegetable stock

2 tablespoons chopped fresh coriander

boiled rice, to serve

Heat the oil in a large, nonstick frying pan. Add the onions, peppers, aubergines, courgettes and mushrooms and cook for 5–6 minutes until all the vegetables are beginning to soften.

Stir in the curry paste and cook, stirring, for 1 minute. Pour in the coconut milk and stock and bring to the boil. Reduce the heat and simmer for 5 minutes. Stir through the coriander and serve immediately with rice.

Slice the bottom off each pepper, then cut down the sides to give 4 or 5 flat, wide slices, leaving the seeds still attached to the core.

Heat a griddle pan and cook the onions on each side for 3 minutes, the peppers on each side for 4 minutes, the aubergine on each side for 3 minutes and the courgettes on each side for 2 minutes. As the vegetables are cooked, arrange them on a large platter.

Make the dressing. Whizz the basil, garlic, oil and vinegar in a small blender. Alternatively, chop the garlic and basil finely, place them in a screw-top jar with the oil and vinegar and shake well to combine thoroughly.

Season the cooked vegetables with sea salt and pepper. Drizzle over the basil dressing, garnish with basil leaves and serve.

TIME 40 MINS
SERVES 4

2 red peppers

1 red onion, cut into 1 cm/¹/₂ inch slices

1 aubergine, cut into 1 cm/¹/₂ inch slices

2 courgettes, cut diagonally in 1 cm/¹/₂ inch slices

sea salt flakes and pepper

basil leaves, to garnish

BASIL DRESSING

large bunch of basil

1 garlic clove, crushed

6 tablespoons olive oil

2 tablespoons white wine vinegar

WARM MIXED VEGETABLE SALAD WITH BASIL DRESSING

Score diagonal cuts on both sides of the fish. Mix the Szechuan pepper with a little salt and rub it over the fish, inside and out.

Heat 2 tablespoons of the oil in a saucepan. Add the shallot and fry gently for 5 minutes or until softened. Stir in the garlic, ginger, sugar and plums and cover with a lid or foil. Cook gently for 10 minutes or until the plums are pulpy but retain a little texture.

Meanwhile, pour the remaining oil into a large frying pan or wok and heat until just smoking. Slide in the fish and cook for 5 minutes, gently moving the fish around by its tail so that it doesn't stick to the base of the pan. Carefully turn the fish and cook for a further 5 minutes or until it is cooked through. Transfer to a warm serving plate.

Add the five-spice paste to the softened plums and stir gently. The plums should be softened and slightly pulpy but not puréed. Spoon the plum sauce over the fish and serve.

TAKES 35 MINS
SERVES 2

625 g/1¼ lb snapper, scaled and gutted

½ teaspoon Szechuan pepper, crushed

150 ml/¼ pint groundnut oil or sunflower oil

1 red shallot, finely chopped

1 garlic clove, crushed

25 g/1 oz fresh root ginger, grated

1 tablespoon light muscovado sugar

500 g/1 lb red plums, halved and stoned

1 teaspoon Chinese five-spice paste

salt

FRIED SNAPPER WITH SPICY PLUM SAUCE

PLOT TO PL

PLUM & AMARETTO TARTLETS

TAKES 20 MINS
SERVES 4

**375 g/12 oz puff pastry, thawed
if frozen**

beaten egg, to glaze

**175 g/6 oz white or golden
almond paste**

**500 g/1 lb red or yellow plums,
halved and stoned**

**4 tablespoons Amaretto liqueur
or brandy**

icing sugar, for dusting

lightly whipped cream, to serve

Lightly grease a baking sheet and sprinkle with water. Roll out the pastry on a lightly floured surface and cut out 6 rounds, each 10 cm/ 4 inches across, using a cutter or small saucer as a guide. Use the tip of a sharp knife to make a shallow cut 1 cm/1/2 inch in from the edge of each round to form a rim. Brush the tops with beaten egg and transfer to the baking sheet.

Roll out the almond paste on a surface dusted with icing sugar and cut out 6 rounds, each 8 cm/3 inches across. Place a round in the centre of each tartlet. Arrange the plum halves over the almond paste, cut sides up, and drizzle with as much liqueur or brandy as the cavities will hold. Bake in a preheated oven, 220°C/425°F/Gas Mark 7, for about 15 minutes until the pastry is well risen.

Spoon over any remaining liqueur and dust with icing sugar. Serve the tartlets with whipped cream.

Put the plums in a small saucepan with 75 g/3 oz of the sugar and the measured water. Cover the pan and heat very gently for about 5 minutes or until the plums are tender but not falling apart. Tip the plums into a sieve set over a bowl to catch the juices and leave to stand.

Meanwhile, make the custard. Whisk the remaining sugar with the cornflour, vanilla extract and egg yolks in a heatproof bowl. Pour the milk into the cleaned saucepan and bring just to the boil. As the milk starts to rise up in the pan, remove it from the heat and pour it over the mixture in the bowl, whisking well.

Carefully tip the custard back into the pan and heat gently, stirring well until thickened and bubbling. Remove the custard from the heat and turn it into a bowl. Leave to stand for 10 minutes.

Arrange the plums in 4 glass dishes and add a tablespoonful of the reserved juice to each one. Use a balloon whisk to whip the cream with the remaining plum juices until slightly thickened. Stir the mixture into the custard until smooth and spoon over the plums.

Scatter each dish with toasted almonds, dust with icing sugar and serve.

TAKES 28 MINS
SERVES 4

500 g/1 lb red plums, quartered and stoned

100 g/3¹/₂ oz golden caster sugar

2 tablespoons water

15 g/¹/₂ oz cornflour

1 teaspoon vanilla extract

3 egg yolks

250 ml/8 fl oz milk

150 ml/¹/₄ pint double cream

1 tablespoon toasted almonds

icing sugar, for dusting

WARM PLUM SUNDAES

PLUM CRUMBLE CAKE WITH CINNAMON CREAM

TAKES 1¼ HRS–1½ HRS
SERVES 8–10

175 g/6 oz unsalted butter, softened

175 g/6 oz caster sugar

3 eggs, lightly beaten

225 g/7½ oz self-raising flour

1 teaspoon baking powder

100 g/3½ oz ground almonds

6 ripe plums, halved and stoned

CRUMBLE

25 g/1 oz plain flour

25 g/1 oz rolled oats

25 g/1 oz unsalted butter, finely diced

50 g/2 oz soft brown sugar

50 g/2 oz chopped almonds

CINNAMON CREAM

200 ml/7 fl oz crème fraîche

1 tablespoon icing sugar, sifted

1 teaspoon ground cinnamon

🍃 Oil and base-line a 24 cm/9½ inch cake tin. Combine the crumble ingredients in a bowl, rubbing the butter in well, and set aside.

🍃 Use an electric mixer to cream together the butter and sugar until pale and fluffy then beat in the eggs a little at a time until creamy. Sift the flour into the bowl with the baking powder, add the ground almonds and fold into the creamed mixture until evenly combined.

🍃 Spoon the cake mix into the prepared tin and smooth the surface with the back of a spoon. Arrange the plums, cut side up, over the top of the cake, pressing them down gently into the mix. Scatter the crumble topping evenly over the plums.

🍃 Bake the cake in a preheated oven, 180°C/350°F/Gas Mark 4, for 50–60 minutes until it is risen. Insert a skewer into the centre; if it comes out clean the cake is cooked. If not, return it to the oven for a further 5 minutes and test again. Remove the cake from the oven, leave to cool in the tin for 15 minutes and then turn out on to a wire rack until it is cold.

🍃 Meanwhile, make the cinnamon cream. Beat the ingredients together until smooth and chill until required. Serve the cake in wedges with the cinnamon cream.

Roll out the pastry dough on a lightly floured surface to a rectangle 2 mm/⅛ inch thick. Cut it into 6 rectangles, each 7 × 12 cm /3 × 5 inches, and put them on a baking sheet. Chill for 30 minutes. Bake in a preheated oven, 200°C/400°F/Gas Mark 6, for 15 minutes until the pastry is puffed and golden. Transfer to a wire rack to cool.

Make the white chocolate cream. Put the cream and vanilla pod in a saucepan and heat gently until the cream reaches boiling point. Remove the pan from the heat and scrape the seeds from the vanilla pod into the cream (discard the pod). Immediately stir in the chocolate and continue stirring until it has melted. Cool, chill for 1 hour until firm and then whisk until stiff.

Split the pastries in half crossways and fill each one with white chocolate cream and some raspberries. Sprinkle with icing sugar before serving.

TAKES 35 MINS, PLUS CHILLING
SERVES 6

370 g/12 oz puff pastry, thawed if frozen

150 g/5 oz raspberries

icing sugar, to dust

WHITE CHOCOLATE CREAM

200 ml/7 fl oz single cream

½ vanilla pod

200 g/7 oz white chocolate, chopped

WHITE CHOCOLATE & RASPBERRY PUFFS

HOME GROW

RASPBERRY MERINGUE CHEESECAKE

TAKES 1½–2 HRS, PLUS CHILLING
SERVES 6–8

175 g/6 oz digestive biscuits, finely crushed

50 g/2 oz butter, melted

½ teaspoon ground cinnamon

FILLING
250 g/8 oz soft cheese

150 ml/¼ pint soured cream

1 teaspoon grated lemon rind

1 tablespoon lemon juice

1 teaspoon vanilla extract

75 g/3 oz caster sugar

1 egg

2 egg yolks

FRUIT TOPPING
375 g/12 oz raspberries, fresh or frozen, thawed if frozen

5 tablespoons redcurrant jelly

MERINGUE TOPPING
2 egg whites

125 g/4 oz caster sugar

🌿 Mix the biscuits with the butter and cinnamon. Press the mixture on to the bottom of a lightly buttered 23 cm/9 inch flan dish. Transfer the biscuit base to the refrigerator to set.

🌿 Meanwhile, make the filling. Beat together the cheese and soured cream, then beat in the lemon rind and juice, vanilla extract and sugar. Beat in the whole egg and egg yolks, and continue beating until the mixture is smooth.

🌿 Pour the filling over the base in the flan dish. Bake in a preheated oven, 150°C /300°F/Gas Mark 2, for 1 hour or until the filling is set. Remove the cheesecake from the oven and leave to cool.

🌿 Arrange the raspberries in a single layer over the filling. Melt the jelly in a small saucepan and spoon it over the fruit. Allow the jelly to cool and set, then cover the cake with foil and chill in the refrigerator for at least 6 hours.

🌿 Make the meringue topping. Whisk the egg whites until stiff. Whisk in half the sugar and continue whisking until the mixture is stiff and glossy. Fold in the remaining sugar with a metal spoon. Spread the meringue carefully over the fruit so that it is completely covered, otherwise the jelly will melt. Level the top of the meringue. Cook the meringue in a preheated oven, 180°C/350°F/Gas Mark 4, for 10 minutes or until the meringue is golden brown. Serve immediately.

RASPBERRY & BLACKBERRY CORDIAL

TAKES 2¾–3 HRS, PLUS STRAINING
MAKES 2 X 500 ML/17 FL OZ BOTTLES

750 g/1½ lb blackberries

750 g/1½ lb raspberries

150 ml/¼ pint water

about 550 g/1 lb 2 oz granulated sugar

Put the blackberries and raspberries in a large bowl and crush them with a potato masher. Stir in the measured water.

Set the bowl over a medium-sized pan, one-quarter filled with boiling water, and cook over a low heat for 1 hour.

Mash the fruit again, then spoon the mixture into a jelly bag suspended over a large bowl and strain for at least 4 hours or overnight.

Measure the cold juice into a large pan and add 375 g/12 oz sugar for every 600 ml/1 pint of liquid. Cook over a low heat, stirring continuously, for about 10 minutes until the sugar has completely dissolved.

Carefully skim off any scum. Transfer the cordial to warm, dry bottles, leaving a headspace of 2.5 cm/1 inch. Add tops and seal loosely.

Stand a small wire rack in the bottom of a deep saucepan and stand the bottles, spaced slightly apart, on the rack. Wedge folded pieces of newspaper between the bottles so that they do not fall over or knock together, then fill the pan with cold water to reach the necks of the bottles.

Put a sugar thermometer to the pan and slowly heat the water over 1 hour to 77°C/170°F. Maintain the temperature for 20–30 minutes, depending on the size of the bottles.

Ladle some of the water out of the pan, then use tongs to lift the bottles out on to a wooden board. Using a cloth, screw the tops on tightly and leave to cool. Label and store in a cool, dark place. The cordial will keep for up to 6 months.

To serve dilute 1 part cordial to 4 parts cold water.

Reserve 4 small strawberries for decoration. Hull the remaining strawberries and use a fork or food processor to mash them with the icing sugar. Pull off the lavender flowers from the stems and crumble them into the strawberries to taste.

Put the yogurt in a bowl, crumble in the meringues then lightly mix together. Add the strawberry mixture, fold together with a spoon until marbled, then spoon into glasses.

Cut the reserved strawberries in half then decorate the desserts with the strawberry halves and lavender flowers. Lightly dust with icing sugar and serve immediately.

TAKES 15 MINS
SERVES 4

400 g/13 oz strawberries

2 tablespoons icing sugar, plus extra to decorate

4–5 lavender flowers, plus extra to decorate

400 g/13 oz Greek yogurt

4 ready-made meringue nests

STRAWBERRY & LAVENDER CRUSH

TAKES 15 MINS, PLUS STANDING
MAKES 2 X 500 M/17 FL OZ BOTTLES

300 g/10 oz strawberries, hulled
and cut into quarters

I tablespoon pink peppercorns
in brine, drained and
roughly crushed

I litre/1³/₄ pints white wine
vinegar

extra strawberries and pink
peppercorns, to decorate

🌿 Put the strawberries into a clean, dry, wide-necked bottle or glass storage jar. Add the peppercorns and top up with the vinegar.

🌿 Seal with an airtight lid and turn the bottle upside down several times to bruise the strawberries slightly and release their flavour.

🌿 Leave in a warm place for 2 weeks, turning the bottle once a day.

🌿 Strain the vinegar into dry bottles and tuck a few extra whole strawberries and peppercorns into the bottles to decorate. Seal with airtight tops, then label and store in a cool, dark place. The vinegar will keep for up to 6 months.

STRAWBERRY & PINK PEPPERCORN VINEGAR

STRAWBERRIES WITH BALSAMIC VINEGAR

TAKES 10 MINS, PLUS CHILLING
SERVES 4

500 g/1 lb strawberries, hulled and halved

2 tablespoons good-quality balsamic vinegar

5 mint leaves, roughly chopped

caster sugar, to taste

200 g/7 oz ricotta cheese

1 tablespoon lemon juice

1 teaspoon clear honey

Gently combine the strawberries, balsamic vinegar and mint in a large bowl. Add sugar to taste, cover with clingfilm and leave to macerate in the refrigerator for 1 hour. Stir gently from time to time to combine the flavours.

Mash the ricotta in a bowl with a fork, stir in the lemon juice and honey. Cover with clingfilm and refrigerate until ready to serve.

Serve the strawberries and their syrup in dessert bowls with a generous dollop of the flavoured ricotta.

Put the blackberries and blackcurrants with the honey in a heavy-based saucepan and cook gently, stirring occasionally, for 10–15 minutes until tender. Add the raspberries and strawberries and leave to cool. Strain the fruit, reserving the juice.

Cut 3 circles of bread the same diameter as a 900 ml/1½ pint pudding basin. Shape the remaining bread to fit round the sides of the basin. Soak all the bread in the reserved fruit juice.

Line the bottom of the basin with one of the circles, then arrange the shaped bread around the sides. Pour in half the fruit and place another circle of bread on top. Cover with the remaining fruit, then top with the remaining bread circle.

Cover the pudding with a saucer small enough to fit inside the basin and put a 500 g/1 lb weight on top. Chill in the refrigerator overnight.

Turn the pudding on to a serving plate and pour over any remaining fruit juice. Decorate with redcurrants and mint sprigs and serve with whipped cream.

SUMMER PUDDING

500 g/1 lb mixed blackberries and blackcurrants

3 tablespoons clear honey

125 g/4 oz raspberries

125 g/4 oz strawberries, hulled and halved

8 slices of wholemeal bread, crusts removed

redcurrants and sprigs of mint, to decorate

whipped cream, to serve

SUMMER FRUIT FLAN

TAKES 50 MINS, PLUS COOLING
SERVES 4

500 g/1 lb puff pastry, thawed if frozen

beaten egg, to glaze

CUSTARD FILLING

1 egg

50 g/2 oz caster sugar

40 g/1½ oz plain flour

300 ml/½ pint milk

25 g/1 oz butter, diced

few drops of vanilla extract

TOPPING

250 g/8 oz strawberries, hulled and sliced

125 g/4 oz raspberries

125 g/4 oz loganberries

250 g/8 oz cherries, stoned and halved

3 peaches, sliced

125 g/4 oz redcurrants, stemmed

125 g/4 oz blackcurrants, stemmed

4 tablespoons redcurrant or bramble jelly

Roll out the pastry on a lightly floured surface to a 30 cm/12 inch square. Place on a greased baking sheet. Trim off a 2.5 cm/1 inch strip from all sides, then brush the edges with egg. Place the strips on top of the pastry, around the edge, to form a case, trimming them to fit. Press down to seal, then pinch the edges to decorate.

Prick the base of the pastry all over with a fork, then brush the edges with egg. Bake in a preheated oven, 220°C /425°F/Gas Mark 7, for 20 minutes, until the pastry is risen and golden brown. Leave to cool on a wire rack.

Make the filling. Put the egg and sugar in a bowl and whisk until frothy. Whisk in the flour and 1 tablespoon milk. Heat the remaining milk in a saucepan. Pour the hot milk into the egg mixture, stirring all the time.

Return the filling mixture to the pan and cook over a moderate heat, stirring, until the custard is thick and smooth. Remove from the heat and beat in the butter and vanilla extract. Cover closely and leave to cool.

Spread the custard over the pastry case and arrange the fruit on top. Warm the jelly in a small pan and brush over the fruit and pastry edges. Leave to set before serving.

WAFFLES WITH BERRY COMPOTE

TAKES 50 MINS
SERVES 2

50 ml/2 fl oz milk

I egg, separated

40 g/1 1/2 oz unsalted butter, melted, plus extra for greasing

50 g/2 oz self-raising wholemeal flour

1 1/2 tablespoons icing sugar, sifted

finely grated rind of 1/4 lemon

BERRY COMPOTE

65 g/2 1/2 oz strawberries, hulled and quartered

65 g/2 1/2 oz raspberries

65 g/2 1/2 oz blueberries

I tablespoon elderflower cordial

2 tablespoons Greek yogurt, to serve

🍃 Make the waffles. Pour the milk into a bowl, add the egg yolk and whisk lightly. Add 2 teaspoons of the melted butter and work in lightly with a fork.

🍃 Heat a waffle iron on the hob or preheat an electric one while you sift the flour into a bowl. Make a well in the centre of the flour and gradually beat in the milk mixture and the remaining melted butter. Whisk the egg white in a separate bowl until stiff moist peaks form, then fold into the batter with 2 teaspoons icing sugar and the lemon rind.

🍃 Grease the waffle iron and pour in about a quarter of the batter. Close and cook for 4–5 minutes, turning once or twice if you are using a hob-top model. When the waffle is golden brown, cover and keep it warm while you cook the remainder.

🍃 Meanwhile, put all the berries and the elderflower cordial in a small saucepan and heat gently until the juices just start to flow.

🍃 Put 2 waffles on each plate and serve with the berries and a spoonful of Greek yogurt.

THE GOOD

TIME 25 MINS, PLUS CHILLING
SERVES 8

50 g/2 oz margarine, melted

125 g/4 oz digestive biscuits, crushed

25 g/1 oz demerara sugar

300 g/10 oz curd cheese

50 g/2 oz caster sugar

2 eggs, separated

grated rind and juice of ½ orange

15 g/½ oz gelatine

300 ml/½ pint whipped cream, whipped

TOPPING

225 g/7½ oz can blackcurrants

2 teaspoons arrowroot

finely grated rind and juice of 1 orange

🌿 Combine the margarine, biscuit crumbs and demerara sugar in a bowl. Spread the mixture over the base of a lightly oiled 20 cm/8 inch loose-bottomed cake tin and chill until firm.

🌿 Put the curd cheese in a bowl and beat in the sugar, egg yolks and orange rind. Soak the gelatine in the orange juice, then heat gently until dissolved. Stir into the curd cheese mixture with the cream.

🌿 Whisk the egg whites until stiff. Fold 2 tablespoons into the curd cheese mixture to soften it. Fold in the remaining egg white and spread evenly over the biscuit base. Chill in the refrigerator until set.

🌿 Drain the blackcurrants and heat the syrup in a small pan. Blend the arrowroot with the orange rind and juice and pour the mixture into the syrup, stirring. Return the pan to the heat and bring to the boil, stirring, until thickened. Add the blackcurrants and allow to cool.

🌿 Remove the cheesecake from the tin and pour the blackcurrant mixture over the top. Cool, then chill until ready to serve.

BLACKCURRANT CHEESECAKE

TAKES 25 MINS, PLUS FREEZING
SERVES 4

500 g/1 lb redcurrants

125 g/4 oz icing sugar, sifted

juice of 1 orange

1 egg white

TO SERVE

frosted currant leaves

clusters of redcurrants

Put the redcurrants, icing sugar and orange juice in a food processor or blender and whizz to a purée. Rub through a sieve to remove the pips and transfer to a rigid freezer container. Cover, seal and freeze for 2–3 hours. Whisk to break up the crystals.

Whisk the egg white until stiff, then whisk it into the half-frozen purée. Return to the freezer until firm. Transfer the sorbet to the refrigerator 15 minutes before serving to soften.

To serve, scoop the sorbet into chilled glasses and decorate with frosted currant leaves and redcurrant clusters.

REDCURRANT SORBET

LAVENDER & REDCURRANT SYRUP

TAKES 2½–2¾ HRS, PLUS
STANDING AND STRAINING
MAKES 3 X 250 ML/8 FL OZ
BOTTLES

1.5 kg/3 lb redcurrants, destemmed

300 ml/½ pint water

12 large fresh or dried lavender heads

about 375 g/12 oz granulated sugar

Put the redcurrants in a saucepan with the measured water and crush with a potato masher. Cover the pan and cook over a low heat for 30 minutes. Take the pan off the heat and crush the fruits again. Add the lavender heads and press them down beneath the liquid. Leave to infuse for 1 hour, then strain the mixture overnight through a jelly bag suspended over a large bowl.

The next day, measure the juice into a large pan and add 375 g/12 oz sugar for each 600 ml/1 pint of juice. Cook over a low heat, stirring continuously, for about 10 minutes until the sugar has dissolved.

Carefully skim off any scum. Transfer the syrup to dry bottles, leaving a headspace of 2.5 cm/1 inch. Add tops and seal loosely. Stand the bottles on a wire rack in a deep pan with newspaper wedged between them to hold them in place. Then fill the pan with cold water up to the necks of the bottles.

Put a sugar thermometer into the pan and slowly heat the water over 1 hour to 77°C/170°F then maintain the temperature for 20–30 minutes depending on the size of the bottles.

Using tongs, carefully lift the jars out of the pan on to a wooden board. Seal the tops and leave to cool. Label and store in a cool, dark place for up to 3–6 months.

🌿 Rinse a large bowl with boiling water, then add the elderflowers and lemon and orange rinds. Cover with the freshly boiled water and press the flowerheads beneath the water, keeping them down if necessary with crumpled, wetted greaseproof paper. Cover the bowl and leave to stand overnight.

🌿 The next day, pour the water, flowers and fruit rinds through a fine sieve or jelly bag suspended over a large bowl. Leave to drip for 30 minutes.

🌿 Pour the liquid into a large pan and add the sugar and lemon juice. Cook over a low heat, stirring continuously, for 10 minutes until the sugar has completely dissolved. Stir in the tartaric acid (this acts as the preservative and means that you do not need to sterilize by simmering in a pan of water).

🌿 Carefully skim off any scum. Transfer the cordial to dry bottles. Seal with airtight lids, then label and leave to cool. Store the cordial in a cool, dark place; it will keep for 2–3 months.

🌿 To serve dilute 1 part cordial with 4 parts chilled still or sparkling water.

TAKES 30 MINS, PLUS STANDING AND STRAINING
MAKES 3 X 500 ML/17 FL OZ AND 1 X 250 ML/8 FL OZ BOTTLES

12 elderflower heads, shaken and picked over

grated rind of 2 lemons

grated rind of 1 orange

1.5 litres/2¹/₂ pints freshly boiled water

875 g/1³/₄ lb granulated sugar

200 ml/7 fl oz lemon juice

25 g/1 oz tartaric acid

ELDERFLOWER & LEMON CORDIAL

GOOSEBERRY & ELDERFLOWER FOOL

TAKES 20 MINS, PLUS CHILLING
SERVES 4

**500 g/1 lb frozen gooseberries,
plus extra to decorate**

**3 tablespoons undiluted
elderflower cordial**

**100 g/3$^{1}/_{2}$ oz caster sugar, plus
extra to decorate**

125 g/4 oz mascarpone cheese

150 g/5 oz ready-made custard

biscuits, to serve

Put the frozen gooseberries in a saucepan with the cordial and sugar and cook, uncovered, for 5 minutes, stirring until softened. Transfer to a food processor or blender and whizz until smooth.

Add the mascarpone and custard and blend briefly until mixed. Press the mixture through a sieve, if liked, then pour the mixture into individual serving dishes. Chill for several hours.

To serve decorate the tops of the fools with a few extra defrosted gooseberries rolled in a little extra sugar. Serve with dainty, crisp biscuits.

GOOSEBERRY FLAPJACK TART

TAKES 1¼ HRS–1½ HRS
SERVES 4–6

PASTRY

175 g/6 oz plain flour

75 g/3 oz chilled butter, diced

1 egg yolk

FILLING

500 g/1 lb gooseberries, halved and stoned

25 g/1 oz caster sugar

2 tablespoons orange juice

50 g/2 oz butter

2 tablespoons golden syrup

50 g/2 oz light muscovado sugar

75 g/3 oz porridge oats

🍃 Make the pastry. Put the flour in a bowl, add the butter and rub it in with your fingertips until the mixture resembles fine breadcrumbs. Stir in the egg yolk and enough cold water, about 2–3 tablespoons, to mix to a firm dough.

🍃 Knead the dough briefly on a lightly floured surface, then roll it out and line a 20 cm/8 inch pie plate. Fill with crumpled foil and bake in a preheated oven, 200°C/400°F/Gas Mark 6, for 15 minutes. Reduce the oven temperature to 180°C/350°F/Gas Mark 4.

🍃 Fill the pie case with the gooseberries and sprinkle with the caster sugar and orange juice.

🍃 Heat the butter, syrup and muscovado sugar in a saucepan, stirring until the butter and syrup have melted to form a smooth sauce. Remove the pan from the heat and stir in the oats.

🍃 Spread the oat mixture over the gooseberries, return the tart to the oven and bake for 25–30 minutes, until the flapjack topping has browned and the gooseberries are tender. Cover the surface with a sheet of foil if the flapjack becomes too brown. Serve warm or cold.

TAKES 1¼ HRS
MAKES ABOUT 1.5 KG/3 LB

1 kg/2 lb gooseberries,
topped and tailed

125 g/4 oz blanched almonds,
halved

175 ml/6 fl oz lemon juice

300 ml/½ pint water

1 kg/2 lb sugar

Put the gooseberries into a pan with the almonds, lemon juice and measured water. Bring to the boil, then reduce the heat and cover the pan. Simmer for 20 minutes until the fruit is soft.

Add the sugar and cook over a low heat, stirring continuously, until the sugar has completely dissolved. Increase the heat and bring to the boil, then boil, uncovered, for 20 minutes, stirring occasionally, until the conserve has thickened to a heavy syrup.

Transfer the conserve to hot jars and cover the surface of each with a disc of waxed paper, waxed side down, then top with an airtight lid or cellophane cover. Label and leave to cool, then store in a cool, dark place. It will keep for 3–4 months.

GOOSEBERRY & ALMOND CONSERVE

AUTUMN

BROCCOLI SQUASHES
PUMPKINS COURGETTES
CUCUMBER BEETROOT
CELERY FENNEL
SWEETCORN APPLES
BLACKBERRIES PEARS

FARE

IN AUTUMN

Autumn is traditionally the time for harvest festivals. Most of the crops will be harvested now, and the beds in your allotment should begin to empty out. Autumn vegetables, including pumpkins, squash, beetroot and broccoli, start to change the way we eat, and we turn from salads and light dishes to heartier fare, such as casseroles and warming vegetable stews. The fruits of autumn, especially apples and pears, make great jams, jellies and chutneys as well as pies and tarts. And don't forget to make the most of blackberries, which make a delicious warm, syrupy sauce to accompany ice cream, and fantastic blackberry and apple crumbles. Think about using some of your sweetcorn, broccoli or pumpkins to make delicious soups that you can freeze ready for the chilly winter months to come.

MAKE THE MOST OF ...

APPLES

In the limited space of an allotment you are most likely to have an apple tree grown as an espalier or cordon to save room. Cup your hand under an apple, lift and twist. If it is perfectly ripe, it will come away easily. Taste apples to see if they are ripe: they should be sweet and juicy and have brown pips. Handle the apples with care and remove any bruised or eaten fruit. To store, wrap them in paper and place in trays. The best way to freeze apples is to stew them first with some sugar.

BEETROOT

Use both the root and the leaves, which make an attractive and tasty addition to salads. Allow the beetroot to grow until it is about the size of a tennis ball and has a good, rich colour. Lift using a garden fork, taking care not to cause any damage. Beetroot can be stored for several months. Remove the leaves and store the bulbs in boxes in a cool, dry place.

BLACKBERRIES

Blackberries can be harvested from late summer through to late autumn. The berries should be plump and deep purple in colour, but the best way to check if they are ready is to taste a couple. They should come away from the plant easily when they are ready. Harvest on a dry day to prevent them getting soggy. They are best eaten fresh, but can be cooked with sugar and frozen.

BROCCOLI

There are so many different types of broccoli that you could have a steady supply all year round. The traditional green-headed broccoli is at its best mid-autumn. The flowering heads should be well developed and plump, but not opened. If you harvest broccoli regularly it should grow sideshoots, which can also be used and extend the harvest season. Store broccoli in the refrigerator or blanch and freeze it.

COURGETTES

A single courgette plant can produce a great yield. Cut the fruit from the plant using a sharp knife, but be careful of the spines on the stems. Courgettes should be harvested while they are still tender and 10–15 cm/4–6 inches long. Store them in a refrigerator for up to a week. The flowers can also be cooked: try them in risottos (see page 173), deep-fried in batter or stuffed.

CUCUMBERS

Cucumbers are often associated with summer salads, but they are at their best during the autumn months. Harvest when they have a good green colour and are plump and firm to the touch. They should be about 25 cm/10 inches long, although different types and cultivars vary in length. Cut the fruit from the plant with a sharp knife. Store cucumbers in a refrigerator for up to 7 days.

PEARS

It can be difficult to know when to harvest pears because they don't ripen well if they are left on the tree. They should be of a good size and still be firm to the touch. The skin should be light green-yellow, and they should come away from the tree easily with a gentle twist. Leave them for up to 3 weeks to ripen.

PUMPKINS

Although pumpkins aren't the tastiest of vegetables, they do make wonderful pies and soups. The fruit should be left on the vine for as along as possible so that it forms a tough skin, which means that it can be stored over the winter, but look out for early frosts and cover the fruit if necessary. Pumpkins should be a good size and rich in colour. Cut them from the vine with a sharp knife, leaving as much stalk on the fruit as possible. Leave for another 10 days before using. Store in a cool, dry place for several months or freeze some cooked mashed pumpkin.

SQUASH

Squash are easier to grow than pumpkins because they take up less room and can be grown over an arch or trellis, creating an attractive and practical display. They are also much more flavoursome than pumpkins, with their sweet, nutty flesh, but they are harvested in the same way (see above).

SWEETCORN

Sweetcorn is at its best in early autumn. Wait for the beard at the end of the husk to turn brown, then test to see if the cob is ripe by peeling back the husk – the corn should be a pale lemon yellow colour. Once it is harvested it should produce a creamy coloured liquid. Eat the corn as soon as possible to ensure the best flavour. Cobs can be stored in the refrigerator for a few days.

BROCCOLI & CHEDDAR CHEESE SOUP

TAKES 1¼ HRS
SERVES 6

50 g/2 oz butter or margarine

1 onion, chopped

1 kg/2 lb broccoli, divided into small florets and stalks peeled and cut into pieces

1 large potato, peeled and quartered

1.5 litres/2½ pints vegetable stock

125 ml/4 fl oz single cream

1 tablespoon lemon juice

1 teaspoon Worcestershire sauce

few drops of Tabasco sauce, or to taste

125 g/4 oz mature Cheddar cheese, grated

salt and pepper

watercress, to garnish

Melt the butter or margarine in a large saucepan. Add the onion and broccoli stalks and cook, covered, for 5 minutes over a moderate heat. Stir frequently.

Add the broccoli florets, potato and vegetable stock to the pan. Bring the mixture to the boil and cook, partially covered, for 5 minutes. Remove six or more florets for garnish and set aside. Season the mixture with salt and pepper and continue to cook over a moderate heat for 20 minutes or until all the vegetables are soft.

Put the mixture in a food processor or blender and whizz, in batches if necessary, until smooth. Transfer the soup to a clean saucepan and add the cream, lemon juice, Worcestershire sauce and a few drops of Tabasco sauce. Simmer for 3–5 minutes. Do not allow the soup to boil or it will curdle.

Just before serving, stir in the grated cheddar and garnish each portion with a floret and some watercress.

Toss the steak slices in the cornflour and season to taste with salt and pepper. Heat the oil in a wok or large frying pan. Add the broccoli and mushrooms and stir-fry for 2 minutes. Add the garlic and ginger and stir-fry for another minute, then push everything to the side of the wok.

Add the steak to the wok and stir-fry for 10 seconds. Then add all the remaining ingredients and bring to the boil, scraping any sediment off the bottom of the pan. Serve immediately with egg noodles.

TAKES 20 MINS
SERVES 4

375 g/12 oz sirloin steak, sliced

1 tablespoon cornflour

3 tablespoons vegetable oil

200 g/7 oz broccoli, broken into small florets

150 g/5 oz shiitake mushrooms, halved

2 garlic cloves, crushed

1 teaspoon grated fresh root ginger

2 tablespoons fermented black beans or black bean sauce

2 tablespoons rice wine or dry sherry

2 tablespoons soft brown sugar

3 tablespoons light soy sauce

100 ml/3 1/2 fl oz beef stock

salt and pepper

egg noodles, to serve

BEEF WITH BROCCOLI, SHIITAKE & BLACK BEAN SAUCE

Heat the oil in a large saucepan. Add the onion and cook until golden brown and softened. Add the milk, flour and herbs and slowly bring to the boil, whisking all the time.

Once the sauce is boiling, reduce the heat and cook for 2–3 minutes or until thickened. Add the tomatoes, season to taste with salt and pepper and mix well.

Add the beans, broccoli and parsley to the sauce and bring to the boil, stirring. Pour into a lightly greased 1 litre/1¾ pint ovenproof dish.

Mix the breadcrumbs with the grated Parmesan or Cheddar and sprinkle over the top. Cook in the centre of a preheated oven, 180°C/350°F, Gas 4, for 20–25 minutes or until the breadcrumbs are golden-brown and the sauce is bubbling. Serve with a salad.

TAKES 50 MINS
SERVES 4–6

1 tablespoon vegetable or olive oil

1 small onion, finely chopped

300 ml/½ pint milk

2 tablespoons plain flour

½ teaspoon dried mixed herbs

4 tomatoes, skinned, deseeded and chopped

425 g/14 oz can butter beans, rinsed and drained

150 g/5 oz broccoli, divided into small florets

2 tablespoons chopped parsley

50 g/2 oz wholemeal breadcrumbs

1 tablespoon grated Parmesan or Cheddar cheese

salt and pepper

green salad, to serve

BROCCOLI & BUTTER BEAN BAKE

BROCCOLI, HAM AND MUSHROOM PIE

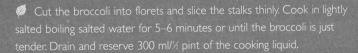

TAKES 1¼ HRS
SERVES 4–6

FILLING

375 g/12 oz broccoli

50 g/2 oz butter

50 g/2 oz plain flour

300 ml/½ pint milk

1 teaspoon wholegrain mustard

125 g/4 oz button mushrooms

125 g/4 oz ham, diced

salt and pepper

PASTRY

175 g/6 oz plain flour

75 g/3 oz butter, diced

75 g/3 oz mature Cheddar cheese, finely grated

milk, to glaze

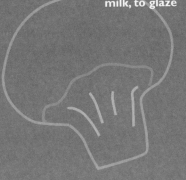

Cut the broccoli into florets and slice the stalks thinly. Cook in lightly salted boiling salted water for 5–6 minutes or until the broccoli is just tender. Drain and reserve 300 ml/½ pint of the cooking liquid.

Melt the butter in a saucepan. Add the flour, stir well and cook for 1 minute. Gradually add the milk and reserved liquid, stirring until you have a smooth sauce.

Stir in the mustard, mushrooms and ham. Season to taste with salt and pepper and simmer for 5 minutes. Remove the pan from the heat and stir in the broccoli. Leave to cool.

Meanwhile, make the pastry. Sift the flour into a bowl. Add the butter and rub in with your fingertips until the mixture resembles fine breadcrumbs. Stir in 50 g/2 oz Cheddar and salt and pepper. Add sufficient water, 3–4 tablespoons, to mix to a firm dough.

Spoon the filling into a buttered 1.5 litre/2½ pint pie dish. Turn the dough on to a lightly floured surface and knead briefly. Roll out the pastry to 5 cm/2 inches larger than the pie dish and cut off a 2.5 cm/1 inch strip all around the edge. Brush the rim of the pie dish with water and press on the pastry strip, cutting it to fit if necessary. Damp the pastry strip and cover with the remaining pastry. Press the edges to seal, then mark all around with a spoon handle or fork.

Brush the pastry with milk and sprinkle with the remaining Cheddar. Cook in a preheated oven, 200°C/400°F, Gas Mark 6, for 25–30 minutes or until the pastry is crisp and golden brown. Serve hot.

VEGETABLE & GARLIC CRUMBLE PIE

TAKES 1¼ HRS
SERVES 4

2 tablespoons oil

1 garlic clove, chopped

1 onion, chopped

2 carrots, chopped

250 g/8 oz broccoli florets

425 g/14 oz can chopped tomatoes

1 tablespoon tomato purée

½ teaspoon dried oregano

1 teaspoon paprika

pinch of sugar

3 tablespoons water

400 g/13 oz can chickpeas, drained

salt and pepper

bread, to serve

CRUMBLE

3 tablespoons olive oil

2 garlic cloves, chopped

75 g/3 oz fresh brown breadcrumbs

2 tablespoons chopped parsley

Heat the oil in a frying pan. Add the garlic and onion and fry for about 5 minutes until softened and lightly coloured. Stir in the carrots and broccoli and mix well.

Add the tomatoes, tomato purée, oregano, paprika and sugar and season to taste with salt and pepper. Add the measured water and bring to the boil, then cover the pan and cook gently for 10–12 minutes or until the vegetables are just tender. Stir in the chickpeas and heat through.

Make the crumble. Heat the oil in a saucepan, add the garlic and fry gently for about 2 minutes until softened. Stir in the breadcrumbs and parsley and season to taste with salt and pepper. Mix well.

Turn the vegetable mixture into a 900 ml/1½ pint ovenproof dish and sprinkle the crumble over the top.

Bake the pie in a preheated oven, 200°C/400°F, Gas Mark 6, for 25 minutes, until the topping is crisp and golden brown. Serve hot with warm bread.

TAKES 35–40 MINS
SERVES 4

175 g/6 oz dried wide rice
noodles

I green chilli, deseeded
and sliced

2.5 cm/I inch fresh root ginger,
peeled and grated

3 tablespoons chopped fresh
coriander

2 teaspoons plain flour

2 teaspoons vegetable oil, plus
extra for frying

STIR-FRIED VEGETABLES

125 g/4 oz broccoli

2 tablespoons vegetable oil

I small onion, sliced

I red pepper, cored, deseeded
and sliced

I yellow pepper, cored, deseeded
and sliced

125 g/4 oz sugar snap peas,
halved lengthways

6 tablespoons hoisin sauce

I tablespoon lime juice

salt and pepper

Cook the noodles in lightly salted boiling water for 3 minutes or until tender. Drain well and transfer to a bowl, then add the chilli, ginger, coriander, flour and oil. Mix well and set aside.

Thinly slice the broccoli stalks and cut the florets into small pieces. Cook the stalks in boiling water for 30 seconds, add the florets and cook for 30 seconds more. Drain.

Heat the vegetable oil in a wok or large frying pan. Add the onion and stir-fry for 2 minutes. Add the peppers and stir-fry for 3 minutes until softened but still retaining their texture. Stir in the cooked broccoli, sugar snap peas, hoisin sauce and lime juice, season to taste with salt and pepper and set aside.

Heat some oil in a frying pan to a depth of I cm/½ inch. Place 4 large, separate spoonfuls of the cooked noodles (half the mixture) in the oil. Fry for about 5 minutes until crisp and lightly coloured. Drain the pancakes on kitchen paper. Keep them warm while you cook the remaining noodle mixture in the same way.

Heat the vegetables through for I minute in the wok or frying pan. Place 2 pancakes on each of 4 serving plates and pile the stir-fried vegetables on top.

RICE NOODLE PANCAKES WITH STIR-FRIED VEGETABLES

PUMPKINS

THE PUMPKIN, WHICH IS SOMETIMES KNOWN AS A WINTER SQUASH, IS A FRUIT RATHER THAN A VEGETABLE. ITS MILD, SWEET FLAVOUR MAKES IT SUITABLE FOR BOTH SWEET AND SAVOURY DISHES. THE SEEDS, FLOWERS AND THE FRUIT ITSELF ARE ALL EDIBLE, AND THE HOLLOWED-OUT SKINS MAKE GREAT HALLOWE'EN LANTERNS, SO NOTHING NEED GO TO WASTE. PUMPKIN GROWING CAN BE FUN AND IS A VERY COMPETITIVE BECAUSE MOST ALLOTMENTS HOLD AN ANNUAL WEIGH-IN, WITH PRIZES FOR THE LARGEST AND HEAVIEST EXAMPLES.

PUMPKINS ARE THOUGHT TO HAVE ORIGINATED IN CENTRAL AMERICA OVER A THOUSAND YEARS AGO, AND THEY WERE INTRODUCED TO EUROPE BY THE SPANISH IN THE 16TH CENTURY. THEY WERE WIDELY USED BY NATIVE AMERICANS AND ALSO BY THE EARLY SETTLERS, AND PUMPKIN PIE (SEE PAGE 164) STILL PLAYS A CENTRAL ROLE IN THE THANKSGIVING CELEBRATIONS.

GOOD FOR YOU

Although the pumpkin is 90 per cent water, it still has many nutritional benefits. It is rich in fibre and low in calories, and it contains vitamins C and E and potassium, all of which help protect against serious diseases. Pumpkin seeds are a good source of fatty acids, protein and iron and zinc.

FIVE OF THE BEST

Becky The classic orange Hallowe'en pumpkin, this is great for carving. The plants produce a good yield.

Rouge Vif d'Etampes This deeply ribbed, orange-red pumpkin has bright orange, well-flavoured flesh. Plants are vigorous growers.

Cushaw This bears smaller, green-striped pumpkins, which are ideal for custards and pies.

Baby Boo Use these miniature pumpkins straight after harvesting.

Crown Prince This blue-grey pumpkin is an ideal vegetable for roasting, and the orange flesh is good in soups.

DELICIOUS IDEAS TO TRY

Seeds Remove the seeds from the pumpkin and wash and dry them. Toss them in a bowl with some olive oil, butter and salt. Spread them on a baking sheet and roast in a hot oven for 15 minutes or until golden and crispy.

Purée Cut the pumpkin in half, remove the seeds and strings. Cut the halves into chunks and steam for 20 minutes. Remove the skin and purée the flesh in a blender.

Chips Remove the seeds and skin and cut the flesh into thin wedges. Drizzle with olive oil and sprinkle with mild chilli powder. Roast in a hot oven for 30 minutes. Serve with ham and eggs.

Mash Mash some cooked potatoes and pumpkin chunks together with a couple of crushed garlic cloves, some crème fraîche and salt and pepper.

Soup Sauté 2 onions with 2 chopped garlic cloves and 2 tablespoons chopped ginger, add 1 kg/2 lb pumpkin chunks, cover with vegetable stock and simmer for 20 minutes. When cool, blend and add a large dollop of double cream. Season to taste and warm through before serving.

TOP TIPS FOR PUMPKINS

Chooser smaller pumpkins, which will be sweeter and have a better flavour.

When harvesting leave the stem on so that the pumpkin will keep for longer.

Pumpkins can be stored for a month at room temperature or for 2–3 months in a cool dry place.

To grow a giant pumpkin leave just one fruit on the vine.

Cut the squash in half and remove all the seeds. Peel off the skin and chop the flesh into small dice.

Heat the butter and oil in a saucepan, add the onion, garlic and squash and sauté for 5 minutes. Add the stock and saffron to the pan, bring to the boil and simmer for 15 minutes.

Pour the soup into a food processor or blender and whizz until smooth. Season generously with salt and pepper.

Return the soup to the pan and reheat gently without letting it boil. Ladle it in to warm bowls and sprinkle each with chopped rosemary and a generous spoonful of grated Parmesan.

TAKES 30 MINS
SERVES 4

1 butternut squash, about 875 g/1^3/$_4$ lb

50 g/2 oz butter

2 tablespoons olive oil

2 onions, chopped

1 garlic clove, crushed and chopped

1 litre/1^3/$_4$ pints chicken or vegetable stock

pinch of saffron threads

salt and pepper

TO SERVE

2 sprigs of rosemary, chopped

75 g/3 oz Parmesan cheese, grated

BUTTERNUT SQUASH SOUP

DIG FOR YO

BABY SQUASH WITH RED BEAN SAUCE

TAKES 40 MINS
SERVES 4

600 ml/1 pint vegetable stock

1 kg/2 lb mixed baby squash, such as gem, butternut or acorn, quartered and deseeded

125 g/4 oz baby spinach

RED BEAN SAUCE

4 tablespoons olive oil

4 garlic cloves, thinly sliced

1 red pepper, cored, deseeded and finely chopped

2 tomatoes, chopped

425 g/14 oz can red kidney beans, rinsed and drained

1–2 tablespoons hot chilli sauce

small handful of coriander, chopped

salt

TO SERVE

steamed white rice

soured cream (optional)

avocado and lime salad (optional)

Put the stock in a large saucepan and bring it to the boil. Add the squash to the pan, reduce the heat and cover. Simmer gently for about 15 minutes or until the squash are just tender.

Meanwhile, make the sauce. Heat the oil in a frying pan. Add the garlic and pepper and fry for 5 minutes, stirring frequently, until very soft. Add the tomatoes, red kidney beans, chilli sauce and a little salt and simmer for 5 minutes until pulpy.

Remove the squash from the stock, reserve the stock and return the squash to the pan. Scatter over the spinach leaves, cover and cook for about 1 minute until the spinach has wilted in the steam.

Pile the vegetables on to steamed rice on serving plates. Stir 8 tablespoons of the reserved stock into the sauce with the coriander. Spoon over the vegetables and serve with soured cream and an avocado and lime salad, if liked.

BEEF & PUMPKIN CURRY

TAKES 2 HRS
SERVES 5–6

75 ml/3 fl oz vegetable oil

1 red pepper, cored, deseeded and cut into chunks

1 green pepper, cored, deseeded and cut into chunks

2 onions, sliced

1 teaspoon ground turmeric

2 tablespoons coriander seeds, lightly crushed

2 teaspoons caster sugar

750 g/1 1/2 lb lean stewing steak, cut into small chunks

3 garlic cloves, sliced

25 g/1 oz fresh root ginger, peeled and finely chopped

1 fresh red chilli, deseeded and chopped

425 g/14 oz can chopped tomatoes

600 ml/1 pint beef or chicken stock

1 kg/2 lb pumpkin, skinned and deseeded

crème fraîche

salt

basmati rice, to serve

Heat the oil in a large, heavy-based saucepan. Add the peppers and cook for 4–5 minutes until they start to colour. Remove with a slotted spoon and set aside. Add the onions, turmeric, coriander, sugar and beef to the pan and cook gently for 5 minutes or until lightly coloured.

Add the garlic, ginger, and chilli to the pan and cook for 2 minutes, stirring. Add the tomatoes and stock and bring slowly to a boil. Reduce the heat, cover with a lid and simmer gently for 1 hour until the beef is tender.

Cut the pumpkin flesh into chunks and add them to the pan with the red and green peppers. Cook gently for 20 minutes until the pumpkin is very soft. Season with salt if necessary and add a little crème fraîche. Serve with basmati rice.

Heat a nonstick frying pan. Add the whole spices and cook over a medium heat, stirring constantly, until lightly browned. Grind to a powder in a spice grinder or in a mortar with a pestle.

Put the pumpkin wedges in a dish. Toss well with the oil, sugar and spice mix to coat evenly. Cook the wedges under a preheated hot grill for 6–8 minutes on each side until charred and tender.

Meanwhile, make the pesto. Put the coriander, garlic, chilli, sugar and pistachio nuts in a food processor and whizz until fairly smooth. Season to taste with salt and pepper and add the coconut cream and lime juice and whizz again. Transfer to a bowl and serve with the pumpkin.

TAKES 25–30 MINS
SERVES 4

1 teaspoon cumin seeds

1 teaspoon coriander seeds

2 green cardamom pods

1 kg/2 lb pumpkin, cut into 1 cm /¹/₂ inch wedges

3 tablespoons sunflower oil

1 teaspoon caster sugar

COCONUT PESTO

25 g/1 oz fresh coriander leaves

1 garlic clove, crushed

1 green chilli, deseeded and chopped

pinch of sugar

1 tablespoon shelled pistachio nuts, roughly chopped

6 tablespoons coconut cream

1 tablespoon lime juice

salt and pepper

SPICED PUMPKIN WITH COCONUT PESTO

Steam the pumpkin for 10 minutes until the flesh is tender. Drain it on kitchen paper to extract the excess liquid, then mash well and set aside to cool for 5 minutes. Soak the saffron threads in boiling water for 5 minutes.

Sift the flour and salt into the bowl of a food mixer and stir in the yeast and sage. Add the pumpkin and saffron liquid. Set the mixer to low and work the ingredients together to form a slightly sticky dough. Increase the speed to high and knead for 5–6 minutes until the dough is smooth and elastic.

Shape the dough into a ball, put it in a lightly oiled bowl, cover with a clean tea towel and leave to rise in a warm place for 1 hour until it has doubled in size.

Turn out the dough on to a lightly floured surface and knock out the air. Shape the dough into a small round and transfer it to a lightly oiled baking sheet. Cover it with oiled clingfilm and leave to rise for a further 30 minutes until it has doubled in size.

Bake in a preheated oven, 200°C/400°F/Gas Mark 6, for 30–35 minutes until the bread is risen and golden and sounds hollow when tapped underneath. Leave to cool on a wire rack.

**TAKES 1 HR, PLUS PROVING
MAKES 1 LOAF**

250 g/8 oz peeled pumpkin, diced

few saffron strands

100 ml/3¹/₂ fl oz boiling water

350 g/12 oz white bread flour

1 teaspoon salt

1 teaspoon fast-action
dried yeast

2 tablespoons chopped sage

PUMPKIN
& SAGE
BREAD

CARAMELIZED PUMPKIN WITH COCONUT RICE PUDDING

TAKES 45 MINS
SERVES 4

175 g/6 oz short-grain rice

425 g/14 oz can coconut milk

250 ml/8 fl oz milk

2 bay leaves

50 g/2 oz caster sugar

400 g/13 oz pumpkin, deseeded

40 g/1 ½ oz unsalted butter

3 tablespoons caster sugar

Put the rice in a heavy-based saucepan with the coconut milk, milk, bay leaves and sugar. Bring it slowly to the boil, stirring. Reduce to the lowest possible heat, partially cover and simmer gently for 30 minutes, stirring frequently, until the rice is tender and the mixture is thickened and pulpy. Add a little more milk if the pudding starts to dry out.

Meanwhile, remove the skin from the pumpkin and cut the flesh into 5 mm/¼ inch slices. Blanch the pumpkin in boiling water for 2 minutes until softened but not falling apart. Drain.

Melt the butter in a frying pan. Add the sugar and cook, stirring, until the sugar dissolves, then cook without stirring until the mixture starts to brown. Add the pumpkin slices and cook gently, turning the pumpkin in the buttery syrup until tender, about 3 minutes.

When the rice is cooked, remove the bay leaves and spoon the pudding into bowls. Top with the pumpkin slices and syrup and serve.

Roll out the pastry on a lightly floured surface and use it to line a round, 25 cm/10 inch, loose-based cake tin at least 3.5 cm/1½ inches deep. Line with greaseproof paper, fill with baking beans inside and bake blind in a preheated oven, 200°C/400°F, Gas Mark 6, for 15 minutes. Remove the paper and weights and bake for a further 5 minutes. Reduce the oven temperature to 180°C/350°F, Gas Mark 4.

Meanwhile, cut away the skin from the pumpkin and roughly chop the flesh. Steam it over a pan of gently simmering water for about 20 minutes until just tender. Remove the pumpkin from the heat and allow it to cool slightly.

Put the pumpkin flesh in a food processor or blender and add the sugar, ginger, cinnamon and eggs. Whizz to a smooth puree. Transfer the mixture to a bowl and stir in the cream. Carefully pour the mixture into the pastry shell and bake for 30 minutes or until the pie is still slightly wobbly in the middle. Dust with icing sugar and serve warm or cold with double cream.

TAKES 1½ HRS
SERVES 10

300 g/10 oz shortcrust pastry, thawed if frozen

1 kg/2 lb pumpkin, deseeded

175 g/6 oz soft brown sugar

2 pieces crystallized ginger from a jar, chopped

1 teaspoon ground cinnamon

2 eggs, beaten

150 ml/¼ pint double cream, plus extra to serve (optional)

icing sugar, for dusting

CLASSIC PUMPKIN PIE

HOME GROW

PUMPKIN SEED & APRICOT MUESLI

TAKES 10 MINS
SERVES 2

50 g/2 oz rolled oats

1 tablespoon seedless sultanas or raisins

1 tablespoon pumpkin or sunflower seeds

1 tablespoon chopped almonds

25 g/1 oz ready-to-eat dried apricots, chopped

2 tablespoons fruit juice, such as apple or orange juice, or water

2 small dessert apples, peeled and grated

3 tablespoons semi-skimmed milk or low-fat natural yogurt

Divide the oats, sultanas or raisins, seeds, almonds and apricots between 2 bowls and pour in the fruit juice or water.

Add the grated apple and stir it in, then top the muesli with milk or yogurt. Serve immediately.

For a softer texture, soak the oats and sultanas or raisins with the fruit juice or water overnight.

COURGETTE & PARMESAN SOUP

TAKES 25 MINS
SERVES 4

25 g/1 oz butter

1 tablespoon olive oil

1 large onion, chopped

475 g/15 oz courgettes, sliced

75 g/3 oz pine nuts

1 tablespoon chopped sage

1 litre/1³/₄ pints vegetable stock

100 g/3¹/₂ oz Parmesan cheese, crumbled

4 tablespoons double cream

salt and pepper

Melt the butter with the oil in a large, heavy-based saucepan. Add the onion, courgettes and pine nuts and cook over a moderate heat for 5 minutes or until softened.

Add the sage and stock and bring to the boil, then reduce the heat, cover and simmer gently for 5 minutes. Add the Parmesan and cook for a further 2 minutes.

Put the soup in a food processor or blender and whizz, in batches if necessary, until partially blended but not smooth, then return to the pan.

Stir in the cream and season to taste with salt and pepper. Reheat gently for 1 minute, then serve in warm soup bowls.

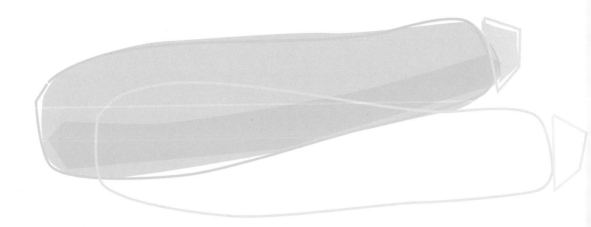

Put the oil, lime rind and juice, garlic, coriander and a little salt and pepper in a polythene bag. Add the courgettes and shake gently in the bag to coat. Seal and set aside until ready to cook.

Heat a ridged frying pan until smoking. Arrange as many courgette slices as will fit in a single layer over the base of the pan and cook for 2–3 minutes until the undersides are browned. Turn the courgettes over and brown on the other side, then transfer them to a warm serving dish while you cook the remainder.

Pour any remaining dressing over the courgettes, sprinkle with chopped coriander to garnish and serve immediately.

TAKES 15 MINS
SERVES 4

1 tablespoon olive oil

finely grated rind and juice of 1 lime

1 garlic clove, finely chopped

2 tablespoons roughly chopped fresh coriander leaves, plus extra to garnish

2 courgettes, about 325 g/11 oz in total, cut into thin diagonal slices

salt and pepper

WARM COURGETTE & LIME SALAD

Make the gremolata. Mix together the lemon rind, oil, chopped parsley and garlic in a small bowl. Set aside.

Heat the oil in a large, nonstick frying pan. Fry the courgette slices over a high heat, stirring, for 10 minutes or until brown. Add the spring onions and cook for 1–2 minutes.

Meanwhile, cook the pasta in a large saucepan of lightly salted boiling water for 10–12 minutes or according to the instructions on the packet until just tender.

Drain the pasta well, then stir in the courgettes, spring onions and gremolata. Serve immediately, topped with Parmesan shavings.

TAKES 27 MINS
SERVES 4

2 tablespoons olive oil

6 large courgettes, thickly sliced

8 spring onions, finely sliced

450 g/14¹/₂ oz dried linguine

Parmesan cheese shavings, to serve

GREMOLATA

grated rind of 2 unwaxed lemons

1 tablespoon oil

10 tablespoons chopped flat leaf parsley

2 garlic cloves, crushed

LINGUINE WITH COURGETTE & GREMOLATA

RIGATONI WITH COURGETTES, FETA & LEMON THYME

TAKES 28–30 MINS
SERVES 4

375 g /12 oz dried rigatoni

3 courgettes, cut into 1 cm/
½ inch slices

6 tablespoons olive oil

2 sprigs of lemon thyme

2 tablespoons lemon juice

200 g/7 oz feta cheese, diced

12 green olives, pitted and
roughly chopped

salt and pepper

Cook the pasta in a large saucepan of lightly salted boiling water for 10–12 minutes or according to the instructions on the packet until just tender. Drain well.

Meanwhile, place the courgettes in a large bowl and toss with 1 tablespoon of the oil. Cook the courgette slices in a preheated ridged grill pan for 2–3 minutes on each side until tender.

Return the courgettes to the bowl, drizzle with the remaining oil, scatter over the lemon thyme and squeeze over the lemon juice. Season with salt and pepper.

Add the hot pasta, the feta and olives to the courgettes. Toss well to combine them and serve immediately.

Put the dried mushrooms in a bowl, cover with boiling water and leave to stand.

Meanwhile, bring a large saucepan of water to the boil with 1 tablespoon oil. Add the pasta sheets, one at a time, and cook for about 4 minutes or according to the instructions on the packet until just tender. Drain each sheet.

Mix together the mascarpone, garlic, dill or tarragon in a small bowl. Season to taste with salt and pepper. Melt half the butter in a frying pan, add the breadcrumbs and fry gently for 2 minutes. Drain on kitchen paper.

Melt the remaining butter in the pan with the remaining oil. Add the fresh mushrooms and courgettes and fry for about 6 minutes until golden. Drain the dried mushrooms, add them to the pan and fry for 1 minute.

Lay 4 pieces of lasagne, spaced slightly apart, in a shallow, ovenproof dish. Spoon over one-third of the vegetables, then a spoonful of the mascarpone mixture. Add another piece of lasagne to each stack and spoon over more vegetables and mascarpone. Finally, add the remaining lasagne, vegetables and mascarpone.

Scatter over the fried breadcrumbs and bake in a preheated oven, 200°C/400°F/Gas Mark 6, for 6–8 minutes until heated through. Serve.

TAKES 30 MINS
SERVES 4

25 g/1 oz dried porcini mushrooms

3 tablespoons olive oil

125 g/4 oz (12 sheets) fresh lasagne, halved

250 g/8 oz mascarpone cheese

2 garlic cloves, crushed

3 tablespoons chopped dill or tarragon

25 g/1 oz butter

40 g/1½ oz breadcrumbs

500 g/1 lb cup mushrooms, sliced

2 courgettes, sliced

salt and pepper

MUSHROOM, COURGETTE & MASCARPONE LASAGNE

LEMON, COURGETTE & TARRAGON BREAD

TAKES 1 HR, PLUS PROVING
MAKES 1 LARGE LOAF

1 courgette, coarsely grated

500 g/1 lb plain flour

finely grated rind of 1 lemon

1 tablespoon chopped tarragon

1 teaspoon sugar

2 teaspoons salt

1 ¹/₂ teaspoons fast-action dried yeast

2 tablespoons olive oil

250 ml/8 fl oz warm water

pepper

Pat the grated courgette dry with kitchen paper. Put the flour in a large bowl and stir in the lemon rind, tarragon, sugar, salt and yeast. Season with pepper to taste. Add the courgette and oil, then mix in enough of the measured water to make a soft dough.

Knead the dough on a lightly floured surface until it is smooth and elastic. Return the dough to the bowl, cover it loosely with oiled clingfilm and leave to stand in a warm place for 1 hour or until it has doubled in size.

Tip the dough on to a lightly floured surface, knead well then transfer to a lightly greased 1 kg/2 lb loaf tin. Cover loosely with clingfilm and leave to stand in a warm place to rise for 30 minutes or until the dough reaches the top of the tin.

Remove the clingfilm and bake the loaf in a preheated oven, 200°C/ 400°F/ Gas Mark 6, for 30 minutes until it is golden brown and sounds hollow when tapped. Check after 20 minutes and cover with foil if it is becoming too brown. Carefully loosen the bread with a spatula and transfer to a wire rack to cool.

TAKES 15 MINS
SERVES 4

750 g/1 1/2 lb courgettes, thickly sliced

75 g/3 oz plain flour

oil, for frying

50 g/2 oz butter

1/2 teaspoon crushed dried chillies

2 garlic cloves, crushed and chopped

juice and rind of 1 lemon

1 tablespoon green olives, pitted and chopped

salt and pepper

🌿 Dust the courgette slices all over with flour.

🌿 Heat some oil in a frying pan. Add the courgettes, in batches, and fry for 2 minutes on each side until golden. Remove from the pan and keep warm.

🌿 When all the courgettes are cooked, pour off the oil from the pan. Add the butter, chillies, garlic, lemon juice and rind and olives and heat until the butter is foaming. Pour over the courgettes, season with salt and pepper and toss to mix. Serve immediately.

COURGETTE FRITTERS

COURGETTE FLOWER RISOTTO

TAKES 40 MINS
SERVES 4

900 ml/1 ½ pints vegetable stock

1 tablespoon olive oil

1 onion, finely chopped

1 garlic clove, finely chopped

275 g/9 oz vialone nano, arborio
or carnaroli rice

150 ml/¼ pint dry white wine

2 large courgettes

4 courgette flowers, cut into
2.5 cm/1 inch strips

grated rind of ½ lemon

1 ½ tablespoons grated Parmesan
cheese

1 tablespoon olive oil

pepper

🌿 Bring the stock to the boil in a saucepan, then reduce the heat to a gentle simmer.

🌿 Heat the olive oil in a heavy-based saucepan over a low heat. Add the onion and cook, stirring occasionally, for 10 minutes until softened. Add the garlic and rice and cook, stirring, for 1 minute. Pour in the wine and cook, stirring, until the liquid has been absorbed.

🌿 Add 2 ladlefuls of hot stock, keeping the heat to a gentle simmer. Stir continuously until the stock has been absorbed and the rice parts when a wooden spoon is run through it.

🌿 Thinly slice one of the courgettes and stir it into the pan. Add another ladleful of stock and continue stirring and adding stock in stages until the rice is creamy and almost tender to the bite. This will take 16–18 minutes.

🌿 Coarsely grate the remaining courgette and stir into the pan with the courgette flowers. Add a final ladleful of stock and cook, stirring, for 1 minute. The rice should now be tender, but still firm.

🌿 Remove the pan from the heat and stir in the lemon rind, Parmesan and oil. Stir vigorously for 15 seconds, then cover the risotto with a tight-fitting lid and leave to stand for 1 minute. Season with pepper and serve immediately.

THAI BEEF & CUCUMBER SALAD

TAKES 30 MINS, PLUS RESTING
SERVES 4

2 lean rump or sirloin steaks, each about 150 g/5 oz, trimmed

150 g/5 oz baby corn cobs

1 large cucumber

1 small red onion, finely chopped

3 tablespoons chopped coriander leaves

4 tablespoons rice wine vinegar

4 tablespoons sweet chilli dipping sauce

2 tablespoons lightly toasted sesame seeds, to garnish

salt

Heat a ridged griddle pan. Put the steaks on the griddle and cook for 3–4 minutes on each side. Allow to rest for 10–15 minutes, then slice the meat thinly.

Put the baby corn cobs into a saucepan of lightly salted boiling water and cook for 3–4 minutes or until tender. Refresh under cold running water and drain well.

Slice the cucumber in half lengthways. Scoop out and discard the seeds with a small spoon and cut the flesh into 5 mm/¼ inch slices.

Put the steak, baby corn cobs, cucumber, onion and coriander into a large bowl. Stir in the vinegar and chilli sauce and mix well. Garnish the salad with sesame seeds and serve.

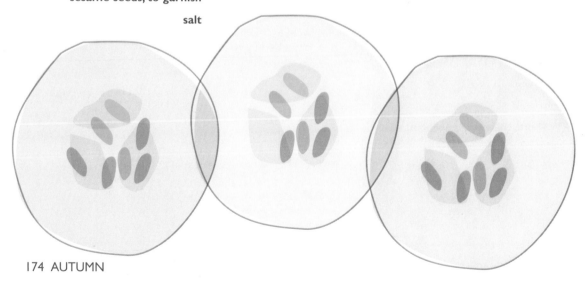

Put the cucumber slices in a colander set over a large plate or in the sink. Sprinkle the salt over the cucumber and leave it to stand for 20–30 minutes, to allow the excess moisture to drain away. Rinse the cucumber under cold running water, then drain thoroughly and arrange the slices in a shallow serving dish.

Make the dressing. Mix together the yogurt, vinegar and dill in a small bowl. Season to taste with pepper.

Spoon the dressing over the cucumber slices and toss lightly to mix. Garnish with dill sprigs and serve.

TAKES 15 MINS, PLUS STANDING
SERVES 4–6

1 cucumber, peeled and very thinly sliced

2 teaspoons salt

sprigs of dill, to garnish

DRESSING

4 tablespoons thick natural yogurt or Greek yogurt

1 teaspoon white wine vinegar

2 tablespoons chopped dill

pepper

CUCUMBER, RADISH & DILL SALAD

Peel the cucumber and cut it into thin slices. Put the slices in a colander set over a large plate or in the sink. Sprinkle the salt over the cucumber and leave to stand for 20–30 minutes, to allow the excess moisture to drain away. Rinse the cucumber under cold running water, then drain thoroughly.

Mix together the sugar, vinegar and dill or tarragon. Toss the cucumber in the herb mixture and chill until ready to serve.

Pile the cucumber salad on to serving plates. Break the trout fillet into large pieces and scatter them over the top with the spring onions. Season lightly with black pepper and serve.

TAKES 15 MINS, PLUS STANDING AND CHILLING SERVES 4

1 cucumber, about 500 g/1 lb

2 teaspoons salt

2 tablespoons caster sugar

4 tablespoons white wine vinegar

3 tablespoons chopped dill or tarragon

250 g/8 oz smoked trout fillet

2 spring onions, finely sliced

pepper

SMOKED TROUT WITH PICKLED CUCUMBER

BORSCHT WITH SOURED CREAM & CHIVES

TAKES 1 HR 25 MINS
SERVES 6

750 g/1 1/2 lb raw beetroot, washed

1 carrot, peeled and grated

1 onion, grated

2 garlic cloves, crushed

1.5 litres/2 1/2 pints vegetable stock

4 tablespoons lemon juice

2 tablespoons sugar

1 large cooked beetroot

salt and pepper

TO GARNISH

150 ml/1/4 pint soured cream

1 teaspoon snipped chives

Scrape young beetroot or peel older ones, then coarsely grate the flesh into a large saucepan. Add the carrot, onion, garlic, vegetable stock, lemon juice and sugar and season to taste with salt and pepper. Bring to the boil, reduce the heat, cover the pan and simmer for 45 minutes.

Meanwhile, cut the whole cooked beetroot into matchsticks about 3.5 cm/1 1/2 inches long. Cover and chill until required.

When the soup vegetables are tender, strain the contents of the pan through a muslin-lined sieve. Discard the vegetables.

Return the soup to the rinsed pan with the beetroot matchsticks. Bring the soup gently to the boil, then simmer for a few minutes to warm the beetroot through. Season the soup to taste with salt and pepper, then ladle it into warm bowls and serve with a spoonful of soured cream and garnished with snipped chives.

Heat the oil in a large, heavy-based saucepan. Add the onion and garlic and fry gently for 3 minutes. Add the rice and cook for 1 minute, stirring.

Add 2 ladlefuls of the hot stock and cook, stirring frequently, until it is almost absorbed. Continue in the same way until all the stock is used and the rice is creamy but still retains a little bite. This will take 18–20 minutes.

Stir in the beetroot, dill, horseradish and nuts. Season to taste with salt and pepper and heat through gently for 1 minute. Spoon the risotto on to plates and serve with mixed salad leaves.

TAKES 30 MINS
SERVES 4

4 tablespoons olive oil

1 large red onion, chopped

3 garlic cloves, crushed

400 g/13 oz risotto rice

1.3 litres/2¼ pints hot vegetable stock

425 g/14 oz cooked beetroot, finely diced

4 tablespoons roughly chopped dill

1–2 tablespoons freshly grated horseradish or 1 tablespoon hot horseradish from a jar

50 g/2 oz salted macadamia nuts or almonds

salt and pepper

mixed salad leaves, to serve

BEETROOT RISOTTO WITH HORSERADISH & MIXED LEAVES

BEETROOT SALAD WITH CORIANDER & TOMATO SALSA

TAKES 20 MINS
SERVES 4

8 cooked beetroots, sliced

2 tablespoons red wine vinegar

I teaspoon caster sugar

2 tablespoons light olive oil

salt and pepper

crème fraîche, to serve

sprigs of coriander, to garnish

TOMATO SALSA

I red onion, finely chopped

425 g/14 oz small vine-ripened tomatoes, deseeded and chopped

2 garlic cloves, crushed

15 g/1½ oz coriander leaves, chopped

Toss the beetroot slices in a bowl with the vinegar, sugar and oil. Season to taste with salt and pepper.

Mix together all the ingredients for the salsa in a separate bowl. Season lightly with salt and pepper.

Arrange about two-thirds of the beetroot slices on 4 serving plates. Pile the salsa on top of the beetroot, then add the remaining beetroot slices. Top with spoonfuls of crème fraîche and spoon over any dressing left in the beetroot bowl. Garnish with coriander sprigs and serve immediately.

Melt 25 g/1 oz of the butter in a large frying pan and fry the cabbage, thyme, caraway seeds, mixed spice and sugar for 10 minutes. Add the wine, port and vinegar and bring to the boil. Cover the pan and cook over a low heat for 20 minutes.

Meanwhile, quarter, core and thickly slice the apples. Melt the remaining butter in a clean frying pan and fry the sliced apples for 4–5 minutes until lightly golden.

Add the apples to the cabbage with the pan juices and the beetroot. Cover the pan and cook for 15–20 minutes until the cabbage is tender. Season to taste with salt and pepper. Stir in the nuts and serve immediately.

CABBAGE, BEETROOT & APPLE SAUTÉ

TAKES 50–55 MINS
SERVES 4

40 g/1 1/2 oz butter

1/2 red cabbage, thinly shredded

1 tablespoon chopped thyme

2 teaspoons caraway seeds

1 teaspoon ground mixed spice

1 tablespoon sugar

150 ml/1/4 pint red wine

2 tablespoons port

2 tablespoons red wine vinegar

2 dessert apples

250 g/8 oz cooked beetroot, diced

50 g/2 oz pecan nuts, toasted

salt and pepper

SPICED BEETROOT

1 tablespoon vegetable oil

2 garlic cloves, finely chopped

1 teaspoon grated fresh root ginger

1 teaspoon cumin seeds

1 teaspoon coriander seeds, coarsely crushed

1/2 teaspoon dried red chilli flakes

625 g/1 1/4 lb freshly cooked and peeled beetroot, cut into wedges

150 ml/1/4 pint coconut milk

1/4 teaspoon ground cardamom seeds

grated rind and juice of 1 lime

handful of chopped coriander leaves

sea salt and pepper

Heat the oil in a large frying pan. Add the garlic, ginger, cumin and coriander seeds and chilli flakes. Stir-fry for 1–2 minutes, then add the beetroot. Fry, stirring gently, for 1 minute, then add the coconut milk, cardamom and lime rind and juice. Cook over a medium heat for 2–3 minutes.

Stir the coriander into the spiced beetroot, season to taste with salt and pepper and serve hot, warm or at room temperature.

BEETROOT & APPLE RELISH

TAKES 2 HRS
MAKES ABOUT 1.5 KG/3 LB

500 g/1 lb cooking apples, peeled, halved and cored

500 g/1 lb raw beetroot, peeled

375 g/12 oz onions, finely chopped

1 tablespoon finely chopped fresh root ginger

2 large garlic cloves, crushed

1 teaspoon paprika

1 teaspoon ground turmeric

1 cinnamon stick

250 g/8 oz soft dark brown sugar

450 ml/³/₄ pint red wine vinegar

Grate the apples and beetroot into a large saucepan, then add all the remaining ingredients.

Bring the mixture to the boil, then reduce the heat and cover the pan. Simmer, stirring occasionally, for about 1½ hours, until the relish has thickened and the beetroot is tender.

Transfer the relish to warm, dry jars and top with airtight lids. Label and leave to mature in a cool, dark place for about 1 week before using, or store, unopened, for up to 9 months.

TAKES 1 HR
SERVES 12

margarine, for greasing

250 g/8 oz self-raising flour

$1/2$ teaspoon ground nutmeg

**$1/2$ teaspoon ground mixed
spice**

**150 g/5 oz light muscovado
sugar**

$1/2$ ripe banana, mashed

**250 g/8 oz cooked beetroot,
peeled and finely grated**

2 small eggs, beaten

125 ml/4 fl oz milk

250 g/8 oz fromage frais

Grease and line a shallow, 20 cm/8 inch, square cake tin. Sift the flour and spices into a large bowl. Stir in the sugar, banana and all but 25 g/1 oz of the beetroot. Make a well in the centre and add the eggs and milk. Beat well, then pour the mixture into the prepared cake tin.

Bake the cake in a preheated oven, 180°C/350°F/Gas Mark 4, for 45 minutes or until a skewer inserted into the centre comes out clean. Allow the cake to cool in the tin for about 10 minutes, then turn it out on to a wire rack to cool completely.

Spread the fromage frais over the cake and scatter the remaining beetroot pieces on the top. Cut the cake into 12 squares and serve.

MOIST BEETROOT CAKE

Butter a large ovenproof dish. Cut the celery heads into quarters lengthways and put them in the prepared dish. Add the oregano, drizzle with olive oil and season well with salt and pepper.

Sprinkle the grated Parmesan over the celery and cook in a preheated oven, 200°C/400°F/Gas Mark 6, for 20 minutes. The celery should become soft and the cheese golden and crunchy on top. Serve immediately.

TAKES 30 MINS
SERVES 4

25 g/1 oz butter
2 small young heads of celery
handful of oregano, chopped
3 tablespoons olive oil
75 g/3 oz Parmesan cheese, grated
salt and pepper

BAKED YOUNG CELERY WITH PARMESAN

FENNEL & LEMON SOUP

TAKES 1 HR
SERVES 4

75 ml/3 fl oz olive oil

3 spring onions, chopped

250 g/8 oz fennel bulb, trimmed, cored and thinly sliced

1 potato, diced

finely grated rind and juice of 1 lemon

900 ml/1 1/2 pints chicken or vegetable stock

salt and pepper

toasted crusty bread, to serve (optional)

BLACK OLIVE GREMOLATA

1 small garlic clove, finely chopped

finely grated rind of 1 lemon

4 tablespoons chopped parsley

16 black Greek olives, pitted and chopped

Heat the oil in a large, heavy-based saucepan. Add the spring onions and cook for 5–10 minutes or until they are beginning to soften. Add the fennel, potato and lemon rind and cook for 5 minutes until the fennel begins to soften.

Pour in the stock and bring to a boil. Lower the heat, cover the pan and simmer for about 15 minutes or until the ingredients are tender.

Meanwhile, make the gremolata. Mix together the garlic, lemon rind and parsley in a bowl, then stir the chopped olives into the herb mixture. Cover and chill.

Whizz the soup in a food processor or blender and pass it through a strainer to remove any strings of fennel. The soup should not be too thick, so add more stock if necessary. Return the soup to the rinsed pan and reheat gently.

Taste the soup and season well with salt, pepper and plenty of lemon juice. Pour it into warm bowls and sprinkle each one with some gremolata, to be stirred in before eating. Serve with slices of toasted crusty bread, if liked.

Pour 300 ml/½ pint of the stock into a large, heavy-based saucepan and add the fennel, onion, courgette, carrot and garlic. Cover the pan and bring to the boil. Boil for 5 minutes, then remove the lid, reduce the heat and simmer gently for 20 minutes or until the vegetables are tender.

Stir the tomatoes into the soup with the beans and sage. Season to taste with pepper and pour in the remaining stock. Simmer the soup for 5 minutes, then allow it soup to cool slightly.

Transfer 300 ml/½ pint of the soup to a food processor or blender and whizz until smooth. Stir the soup back into the pan and heat through gently. Pour it into warm bowls and serve with crusty bread.

FENNEL & BUTTER BEAN SOUP

TAKES 1 HR
SERVES 4

900 ml/1½ pints vegetable stock

2 fennel bulbs, trimmed, cored and chopped

1 onion, chopped

1 courgette, chopped

1 carrot, chopped

2 garlic cloves, finely sliced

6 tomatoes, skinned and finely chopped, or 400g/ 13 oz can tomatoes

2 x 400 g/13 oz cans butter beans, rinsed and drained

2 tablespoons chopped sage

pepper

crusty bread, to serve

Bake the potatoes in a preheated oven, 200°C/ 400°F/Gas Mark 6, for 1 hour or until tender.

While they are still hot, carefully peel the potatoes. Lightly mash the potato and beat in the egg, egg yolk and enough of the flour to form a soft, slightly sticky dough.

Bring a large saucepan of lightly salted water to a rolling boil. Roll small pieces of the potato dough in your hands, drop them into the boiling water and cook in batches for 4–5 minutes until they rise to the surface. Use a slotted spoon to lift out the gnocchi and transfer them to an oiled baking dish. Repeat with the remaining mixture.

Make the sauce. Whisk together the oil, measured water, lemon juice and fennel fronds and season to taste with salt and pepper.

Pour the sauce over the gnocchi and heat them through in a preheated oven, 190°C/ 375°F/Gas Mark 5, for 6–8 minutes until bubbling. Serve immediately sprinkled with grated Parmesan.

TAKES 2 HRS
SERVES 4

1 kg/2 lb floury potatoes

1 egg

1 egg yolk

175 g/6 oz plain flour

grated Parmesan cheese, to serve

FENNEL SAUCE

4 tablespoons olive oil

2 tablespoons boiling water

1 tablespoon lemon juice

2 tablespoons chopped fennel fronds

salt and pepper

POTATO GNOCCHI WITH FENNEL SAUCE

MASCARPONE CHICKEN WITH FENNEL

TAKES 1 HR
SERVES 4

200 g/7 oz mascarpone cheese

small handful of chervil, chopped

2 spring onions, finely chopped

2 garlic cloves, crushed

4 boneless, skinless chicken breasts

40 g/1¹/₂ oz butter

250 g/8 oz fennel bulb, thickly sliced

100 ml/3¹/₂ fl oz white wine

40 g/1¹/₂ oz breadcrumbs

salt and pepper

Beat the mascarpone with the chervil, spring onions and garlic and season with salt and pepper. Make a horizontal slit through the centre of each chicken breast and use half the mascarpone mixture as a stuffing, packing it into the chicken with a teaspoon.

Melt half the butter in a large, heavy-based frying pan and fry the fennel until it is lightly browned. Lift it out with a slotted spoon and transfer it to a shallow, ovenproof dish. Fry the chicken breasts on both sides and place them over the fennel. Spread the remaining mascarpone mixture on top.

Heat the wine in the pan until it bubbles and pour it around the chicken. Wipe out the pan, melt the remaining butter and use it to coat the breadcrumbs.

Sprinkle the breadcrumbs over the chicken breasts and bake them in a preheated oven, 180°C/350°F/Gas Mark 4, for about 30 minutes until cooked through. Serve immediately.

BAKED AUTUMN ROOTS WITH MIXED SPICES

TAKES 50–55 MINS
SERVES 6

1 teaspoon fennel seeds

1 teaspoon cumin seeds

1 teaspoon coriander seeds

$^1/_2$ teaspoon turmeric

$^1/_2$ teaspoon paprika

2 garlic cloves, chopped

3 tablespoons olive oil

500 g/1 lb butternut squash, peeled, halved, deseeded and thickly sliced

4 small parsnips, about 425 g/ 14 oz in total, cut into quarters

3 carrots, about 300 g/10 oz in total, cut into thick strips

salt and pepper

🌿 Crush the seeds using a pestle and mortar or use the end of a rolling pin. Turn them into a large plastic bag and add the turmeric, paprika, garlic, oil and salt and pepper. Fasten the bag and shake to mix the spices together.

🌿 Add the vegetables to the plastic bag, grip the top edge to seal and toss together until the vegetables are coated with the spices.

🌿 Tip the vegetables into a roasting tin and bake in a preheated oven, 200°C/400°F/Gas Mark 6, for 35–40 minutes, turning once, until browned and tender. Transfer to a serving dish.

TAKES 1 HR
SERVES 4

800 g/1 lb 10 oz tuna fillets, cut into bite-sized pieces

4 tablespoons olive oil

2 red onions, halved and thinly sliced

4 garlic cloves, thinly sliced

3 ripe tomatoes, skinned, deseeded and chopped

2 bay leaves

1 red pepper, cored, deseeded and diced

1 tablespoon pimentón dulce (mild paprika)

625 g/1¼ lb potatoes, peeled and cut into bite-sized pieces

salt and pepper

TO GARNISH

chopped flat leaf parsley

capers

Arrange the tuna in a shallow bowl in a single layer and season to taste with salt and pepper. Cover and set aside.

Heat the oil in a saucepan. Add the onions and garlic and cook over a medium heat, stirring frequently, for 8–10 minutes until soft.

Add the tomatoes, bay leaves, red pepper, pimentón and potatoes and stir to mix well. Add enough water to just cover all the ingredients and bring to the boil. Reduce the heat and simmer gently for 25–30 minutes or until the potatoes are tender.

Add the fish, return to the boil and cook for 4–5 minutes.

Taste and adjust the seasoning if necessary. Ladle the stew into warm shallow bowls, garnish with chopped parsley and capers and serve immediately.

FISH & POTATO STEW

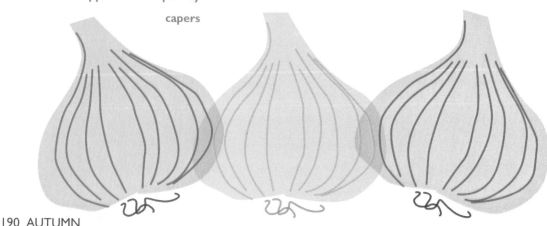

Put 150 ml/¼ pint of the water in a saucepan and bring to the boil. Add the clams, cover with a tight-fitting lid and cook for 4–5 minutes or until the shells have opened. Lift out the clams, reserving the cooking juices, and discard any clams that remain closed. Remove the flesh from the shells and chop it into small pieces.

Put the pork and onion in a large saucepan with a knob of the butter and fry gently for 10 minutes or until browned. Stir in the remaining butter until melted. Add the flour and cook, stirring, for 1 minute.

Add the clam cooking juices, the remaining water, the tomatoes, potatoes and bay leaves. Bring just to the boil, then reduce the heat, cover and cook very gently for 15 minutes or until the potatoes are tender.

Stir in the clams and parsley and cook very gently for 2 minutes. Add the Tabasco sauce and cream, heat through and serve.

TAKES 1¼ HRS
SERVES 4

600 ml/1 pint water

1 kg/2 lb clams, cleaned

200 g/7 oz salt pork, finely chopped

1 large onion, chopped

15 g/½ oz butter

1 tablespoon plain flour

4 tomatoes, skinned and chopped

350 g/11½ oz potatoes, diced

2 bay leaves

3 tablespoons chopped parsley

2 teaspoons Tabasco sauce

150 ml/¼ pint single cream

CLAM CHOWDER

WHOLE BARBECUED SWEETCORN WITH SKORTHALIA

TAKES 45–55 MINS
SERVES 4

4 whole corn cobs, with husks

SKORTHALIA

50 g/2 oz fresh white breadcrumbs

75 g/3 oz ground almonds

4 garlic cloves, crushed

2 tablespoons lemon juice

150 ml/¼ pint olive oil

salt and pepper

Make the skorthalia. Put the breadcrumbs into a bowl and cover with water. Soak for 5 minutes, then squeeze out the excess liquid and transfer the crumbs to a food processor or blender. Add the ground almonds, garlic and 1 tablespoon lemon juice and whizz until mixed. With the motor running, gradually add the olive oil in a thin, steady stream until the mixture resembles mayonnaise. Add more lemon juice if required and season to taste with salt and pepper.

Pull down the outer leaves of the sweetcorn husks and remove the inner silks, then pull the leaves back over the corn kernels. Place the cobs on a barbecue grill over hot coals and cook for about 30–40 minutes until the kernels are juicy and easily come away from the core. When they are ready pull back the leaves of the cobs and spread with skorthalia.

Make the chilli jam. Put all the ingredients in a small saucepan, bring to the boil, then reduce the heat and simmer for 15 minutes. The mixture should be thick, sticky and jam-like, and will become more so as it cools.

Meanwhile, put the lime leaves, flour, egg, Thai fish sauce, lime juice and half the sweetcorn kernels into a food processor or blender and whizz until fairly smooth.

Transfer the puréed mixture to a bowl and stir in the remaining sweetcorn. Heat 5 cm/2 inches oil in a wok and deep-fry teaspoons of the batter, in batches, for 1–2 minutes, until golden. Drain the cakes on kitchen paper and keep them warm while you are cooking the remainder.

Place a sweetcorn cake in each chicory spear, top with chilli jam and some herbs and serve immediately.

SWEETCORN CAKES

TAKES 29 MINS
MAKES ABOUT 24

4 lime leaves, very thinly shredded

65 g/2¹/₂ oz self-raising flour

I egg

I tablespoon Thai fish sauce

I tablespoon lime juice

150 g/5 oz sweetcorn kernels

vegetable oil, for deep-frying

24 chicory spears, about 2 heads

sprigs of coriander, basil and mint, to garnish

CHILLI JAM

125 g/4 oz fresh chillies, deseeded and chopped

I garlic clove, crushed

I onion, chopped

5 cm/2 inches fresh root ginger, peeled and chopped

125 ml/4 fl oz white wine vinegar

500 g/1 lb caster sugar

SWEETCORN RELISH

TAKES 45 MINS, PLUS COOLING
MAKES ABOUT 1.5 KG/3 LB

4 tablespoons corn oil

2 large onions, finely chopped

I green pepper, cored, deseeded
and finely chopped

I red pepper, cored, deseeded
and finely chopped

4 celery sticks, finely chopped

I teaspoon salt

I large garlic clove, crushed

2 carrots, peeled and diced

50 g/2 oz sugar

2 teaspoons mustard powder

750 g/1 1/2 lb frozen sweetcorn

450 ml/3/4 pint vinegar

Heat the oil in a large frying pan. Add the onions, peppers and celery and fry them until they are soft but not browned, then add the salt and garlic.

Add all the remaining ingredients to the pan and bring the mixture to the boil. Reduce the heat and cook, uncovered, for 15 minutes, stirring occasionally.

Transfer the relish to warm, dry jars, pressing the vegetables well down into the juices, then top with airtight lids and leave to cool.

This relish does not need time to mature, but if not immediately consumed, label and store in a cool, dark place for up to 6 months.

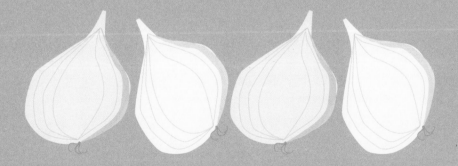

CORNBREAD

TAKES 50–55 MINS
SERVES 8

1 large egg

200 g/7 oz natural yogurt

25 g/1 oz butter, melted, plus extra for greasing

125 g/4 oz fine cornmeal

50 g/2 oz plain flour

1 tablespoon baking powder

1 teaspoon salt

pinch of cayenne pepper

1 large red chilli, deseeded and finely chopped

4 spring onions, finely sliced

125 g/4 oz can sweetcorn kernels, rinsed and drained

50 g/2 oz Parmesan cheese, grated

Lightly grease and line the base of an 18 cm/7 inch square cake tin with nonstick baking paper. Whisk the egg in a bowl until frothy, then stir in the yogurt and melted butter.

Stir in the cornmeal, flour, baking powder, salt and cayenne pepper. Add the chilli, spring onions, sweetcorn kernels and Parmesan and mix thoroughly.

Turn the mixture into the prepared tin and bake in a preheated oven, 180°C/350°F/Gas Mark 4, for 35–40 minutes or until a skewer inserted into the centre comes out clean.

Allow the bread to cool in the tin for 10 minutes, then turn it out onto a wire rack. When the bread is completely cold cut it into squares to serve.

APPLES

JUST A SINGLE APPLE TREE ON AN ALLOTMENT CAN PROVIDE YOU WITH AN ABUNDANCE OF FRUIT FROM LATE SUMMER THROUGH TO AUTUMN, BUT REMEMBER THAT IF YOU ARE GOING TO PLANT A NEW TREE YOU MUST BE SURE THAT THERE IS ANOTHER APPLE TREE NEARBY TO ACT AS A POLLINATOR. THERE ARE NUMEROUS EXCELLENT CULTIVARS, BOTH DESSERT AND COOKING TYPES, THAT CAN BE GROWN ON ROOTING STOCK THAT WILL KEEP THE MATURE TREE TO A MANAGEABLE SIZE. OTHERWISE, TRAIN YOUR APPLE AS A CORDON OR ESPALIER TO SAVE SPACE.

IT IS THOUGHT THAT THE APPLE ORIGINATED IN ASIA THOUSANDS OF YEARS AGO. THERE ARE NOW MORE THAN 7,500 DIFFERENT CULTIVARS, AND THE APPLE REMAINS THE WORLD'S MOST POPULAR FRUIT.

GOOD FOR YOU

The old saying 'an apple a day keeps the doctor away' is not too far from the truth, and there is much evidence that eating apples regularly is good for your health. An apple contains vitamin C and antioxidants that will help protect against serious diseases. Apples are also low in cholesterol and high in fibre. Eating cooked apple is thought to be help if you are suffering from diarrhoea. And with only 50 calories, the apple makes a healthy, filling snack.

FIVE OF THE BEST

Cox's Orange Pippin Thought to be the best of the English apples, pick them in early to mid-autumn and dry store for a month to ensure they are at their best.

Russet An apple with a rough, brown-gold skin, this has an unusual dry taste, which isn't for everyone.

Lord Lambourne This traditional apple has a green skin with red stripes. It is juicy and sweet and appeals to everyone.

Scrumptious This relatively new cultivar produces sweet, crisp fruits. Pick and eat them in early autumn.

Elstar A red-flushed apple that is ready in mid-autumn. The fruits are crisp, juicy and delicious.

DELICIOUS IDEAS TO TRY

Toffee Dip your apple in a syrup made from 250 g/8 oz sugar, 25 g/1 oz butter, 2 tablespoons golden syrup and 125 ml/4 fl oz water. Leave to harden on a baking tray.

Toddy Warm some apple juice in a pan with a couple of sticks of cinnamon, some ground nutmeg, 3 cloves and some orange peel. Whisky is an optional extra.

Salad Try a salad of apples, chopped walnuts and blue cheese served on a bed of salad leaves. Dress with olive oil, lemon juice and Dijon mustard.

Baked Core 4 apples and place them on a baking sheet. Fill the centres with a mixture of brown sugar, some sultanas or currants and a knob of butter. Put a little water in the tray and bake in a hot oven for 45 minutes.

Stewed Peel, core and chop 3 cooking apples. Cover with water and cook on a medium-low heat for about 45 minutes. Add sugar and cinnamon to taste.

TOP TIPS FOR APPLES

🍃 Stop apple flesh from turning brown by adding a squirt of lemon juice.

🍃 After harvesting wrap your apples in paper and store them in crates for a few weeks to allow them to sweat and lose any excess water.

🍃 To freeze apples it is best to blanch them first. Divide the cooked fruit into portions and store them in plastic bags in the freezer.

Make the apricot glaze. Put the jam in a small saucepan with the lemon juice and water and heat gently until the jam melts. Increase the heat and boil for 1 minute, then remove from the heat and press through a fine sieve. Set aside.

Divide the pastry into 4 equal pieces and roll each out on a lightly floured surface until 2 mm/ ⅛ inch thick. Cut out 4 rounds, each 14 cm/ 5½ inches across, using a saucer or plate as a guide. Put the rounds on a lightly oiled baking sheet. Place a slightly smaller plate on each pastry and score around the edge to create a 1 cm/½ inch border. Prick the centres with a fork and chill for 30 minutes.

Arrange the apples slices in a circle over the pastry rounds and scatter over the sugar. Grate over the butter and bake in a preheated oven, 220°C/425°F/Gas Mark 7, for 25–30 minutes until the pastry and apples are golden.

Reheat the apricot glaze until it is warm and brush some over each tart while it is still warm. Serve with ice cream.

TAKES 45–50 MINS, PLUS CHILLING
SERVES 4

375 g/12 oz puff pastry, thawed if frozen

ice cream, to serve

APRICOT GLAZE

125 g/4 oz apricot jam

1 teaspoon lemon juice

1 teaspoon water

APPLE TOPPING

2 Granny Smith apples, peeled, cored and sliced

1 tablespoon caster sugar

25 g/1 oz chilled unsalted butter

FRENCH APPLE FLAN

TOFFEE APPLE BAKE

TAKES 30 MINS
SERVES 4

3 dessert apples, cored and thickly sliced

100 g/3^1/$_2$ oz self-raising flour, plus 1 tablespoon extra

125 g/4 oz light muscovado sugar

50 g/2 oz caster sugar

^{1}/$_2$ teaspoon ground mixed spice

1 egg

100 ml/3^1/$_2$ fl oz natural yogurt

50 g/2 oz unsalted butter, melted

Toss the apple slices in a shallow, ovenproof dish with 1 tablespoonful flour and the muscovado sugar.

Mix 100 g/3½ oz flour with the caster sugar and mixed spice in a bowl. Add the egg, yogurt and butter and stir lightly until only just combined.

Spoon the mixture over the prepared apples and bake in a preheated oven, 220°C/425°F/Gas Mark 7, for about 15–20 minutes until just firm and golden. Serve warm.

Put the rose hips and 300 ml/½ pint water in a saucepan, bring to the boil, cover and simmer for 45–50 minutes.

Meanwhile, place the apples and the remaining water in another pan, bring to the boil, cover and simmer until reduced to a pulp.

Allow both pans of fruit to cool, then strain each one overnight in its own jelly bag suspended over a large bowl.

Mix together the two resulting juices, measure them, then pour into a clean pan. Add 500 g/1 lb sugar and the juice of 1 lemon for each 600 ml/ 1 pint of juice, then stir over a low heat until the sugar has completely dissolved. Increase the heat and boil hard to setting point. Carefully skim off any scum.

Transfer the jelly to warm, dry jars. Cover the surface of each one with a disc of waxed paper, waxed side down, then top with an airtight lid. Leave to cool, then store in a cool, dark place. It will keep for 3–4 months.

**TAKES 1¼ HR, PLUS STRAINING
MAKES ABOUT 2 LB/1 KG**

500 g/1 lb rose hips

600 ml/1 pint water

**1 kg/2 lb cooking apples,
roughly chopped**

sugar

lemon juice

ROSE HIP & APPLE JELLY

LOCAL SEASO

APPLE FRITTERS WITH BLACKBERRY SAUCE

TAKES 40–45 MINS
SERVES 4

2 eggs

125 g/4 oz plain flour

4 tablespoons caster sugar

150 ml/¹/₄ pint milk

sunflower oil, for deep frying

4 dessert apples, cored and thickly sliced

150 g/5 oz frozen blackberries

2 tablespoons water

sifted icing sugar, for dusting

Separate one egg and put the white into one bowl and the yolk and the whole egg into a second bowl. Add the flour and half the sugar to the second bowl. Whisk the egg white until softly peaking, then use the same whisk to beat the flour mixture until smooth, gradually whisking in the milk. Fold in the egg white.

Pour the oil into a saucepan until it comes one-third of the way up, then heat to 190°C/375°F or until a drop of batter bubbles instantly when added. Add a few apple slices to the batter and turn gently to coat. Lift out one slice at a time and lower carefully into the oil. Cook in batches for 2–3 minutes, turning until evenly golden. Lift out with a slotted spoon and drain on kitchen paper.

Meanwhile, put the blackberries, remaining sugar and the measured water into a small saucepan and heat for 2–3 minutes until hot. Arrange the fritters on serving plates, spoon the blackberry sauce around and dust with a little sifted icing sugar.

NAL, ORGANIC

BLACKBERRY & APPLE JAM

TAKES 1½ HRS, PLUS STANDING
MAKES ABOUT 3.25 KG/7 LB

**I kg/2 lb slightly under-ripe
blackberries, stalks discarded**

1.75 kg/3½ lb sugar

I kg/2 lb cooking apples

300 ml/½ pint water

125 ml/4 fl oz lemon juice

Layer the blackberries in a large bowl with the sugar and leave to stand overnight.

Peel, core and slice the apples. Place all the trimmings in a pan and pour in the water. Bring to the boil and boil, uncovered, for about 20 minutes until most of the water has evaporated and the trimmings are pulpy. Press the mixture through a fine sieve into a large pan.

Add the apple slices to the pan and pour in the blackberries with all their juice and any undissolved sugar. Heat the mixture gently to simmering point, stirring continuously for about 10 minutes until the sugar has completely dissolved and the fruit is soft. Add the lemon juice.

Bring the jam to the boil and boil hard to setting point. Remove from the heat and carefully skim off any scum.

Transfer the jam to warm, dry jars. Cover the surface of each one with a disc of waxed paper, waxed side down, then top with an airtight lid or cellophane cover. Label and leave to cool, then store in a cool, dark place. The jam will keep for 3–4 months.

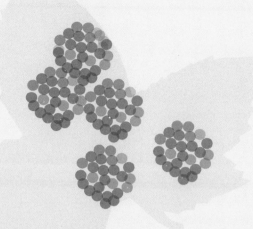

TAKES 45–50 MINS
SERVES 4

500 g/1 lb blackberries

50 g/2 oz caster sugar

1 tablespoon lemon juice

BATTER

1 egg

50 g/2 oz light muscovado
sugar

50 g/2 oz butter, melted

4 tablespoons milk

125 g/4 oz self-raising flour

1 teaspoon ground cinnamon

Mix the blackberries, sugar and lemon juice in a buttered 900 ml/ 1½ pint ovenproof dish.

Make the batter. Beat the egg and sugar in a bowl. Stir in the melted butter and milk. Sift the flour and cinnamon into the bowl and fold in lightly to form a smooth batter.

Pour the batter over the blackberries and bake in a preheated oven, 180°C/350°F/Gas Mark 4, for 25–30 minutes until the topping is firm and blackberries tender. Serve warm.

BLACKBERRY BATTER PUDDING

Sift the flour and salt into a mixing bowl and rub in the butter with your fingertips until the mixture resembles fine breadcrumbs. Stir in the sugar and gradually work in the egg yolk and 1–2 tablespoons cold water to form a soft dough. Knead lightly, wrap and chill for 30 minutes.

Roll out the pastry on a lightly floured surface and use it to line a greased 23 cm/9 inch fluted flan tin. Prick the base and chill for a further 20 minutes.

Line the pastry case with nonstick baking paper and baking beans and place in a preheated oven, 220°C/425°F/Gas Mark 7, for 10 minutes. Remove the paper and beans and bake for a further 10–12 minutes until the pastry is crisp and golden. Reduce the oven temperature to 180°C/350°F/Gas Mark 4.

Make the filling while the pastry case is baking. In a bowl beat together the butter and sugar until pale and light and then gradually beat in the eggs, a little at a time, until incorporated. Lightly beat in all the remaining ingredients, except the pears. Pour the mixture into the pastry case.

Peel and halve the pears and scoop out the cores. Thinly slice each pear lengthways without changing the shape of the pears, then use a palette knife to transfer them to the pastry case, arranging them neatly on the filling. Bake for 55–60 minutes until golden and firm in the middle. Serve warm.

PEAR & CARDAMOM FLAN

TAKES 1½–1¾ HRS, PLUS CHILLING
SERVES 6

175 g/6 oz plain flour

¼ teaspoon salt

100 g/3½ oz unsalted butter, diced, plus extra for greasing

2 tablespoons caster sugar

1 egg yolk

FILLING

125 g/4 oz unsalted butter, softened

75 g /3 oz caster sugar

2 small eggs, lightly beaten

75 g/3 oz ground hazelnuts

25 g/1 oz ground rice

seeds from 2 cardamom pods, crushed

1 teaspoon grated lemon rind

4 tablespoons soured cream

3 small firm pears

PEAR & CHOCOLATE CRUMBLE

50 g/2 oz light muscovado sugar

150 ml/¼ pint water

25 g/1 oz raisins

½ teaspoon ground cinnamon

4 ripe dessert pears, peeled, halved and cored

40 g/1½ oz unsalted butter

50 g/2 oz porridge oats

25 g/1 oz hazelnuts, roughly chopped

50 g/2 oz plain dark or milk chocolate, chopped

lightly whipped cream or Greek yogurt, to serve (optional)

Put half the sugar in a large frying pan with the measured water, raisins and cinnamon. Bring just to the boil then add the pears. Reduce the heat and gently simmer the pears for 5 minutes or until they are slightly softened.

Meanwhile, melt the butter in a separate frying pan or saucepan. Add the porridge oats and cook gently for 2 minutes. Stir in the remaining sugar and cook over a low heat until golden.

Spoon the pears on to serving plates. Stir the hazelnuts and chocolate into the oat mixture. Once the chocolate starts to melt, spoon it over the pears. Serve the crumble topped with whipped cream or Greek yogurt, if liked.

Melt the butter in a small saucepan. Remove it from the heat and stir in the honey. Sprinkle the pear slices with a little lemon juice as soon as they are prepared to prevent discoloration. Line a baking sheet with foil and lay the pear slices on it.

Brush the pears with the butter and honey mixture and cook them under a preheated hot grill for 5 minutes.

Meanwhile, make the minted mascarpone. Lightly whisk the mint and granulated sugar into the mascarpone in a bowl.

Divide the pear slices among 4 plates and add a dollop of the minted mascarpone. Decorate each portion with a mint sprig, then lightly dust with icing sugar and cinnamon and serve immediately.

TAKES 20 MINS
SERVES 4

30 g/1¼ oz unsalted butter

2 tablespoons clear honey

4 ripe dessert pears, such as Red William, cored and sliced lengthways

lemon juice, for sprinkling

MINTED MASCARPONE

1 tablespoon finely chopped mint

1 tablespoon granulated sugar

175 g/6 oz mascarpone cheese

TO DECORATE

sprigs of mint

sifted icing sugar

ground cinnamon

PEARS WITH MINTED MASCARPONE

ORCHARD FRUITS WITH MUSCAT WINE & BAY CREAM

TAKES 50–52 MINS, PLUS CHILLING
SERVES 6

200 ml/7 fl oz double cream

6 bay leaves

3 small pears

3 small sweet dessert apples

250 ml/8 fl oz Muscat (sweet white) wine

pared rind, cut into thin strips, and juice of $^1/_2$ orange

2 teaspoons clear honey

Pour the cream into a small saucepan, add 3 of the bay leaves and bring the cream just to the boil. Remove the pan from the heat, allow the cream to cool then chill for 2 hours.

Peel the pears and apples and cut them in half, cutting down through the stalks too. Carefully scoop the cores away with a small spoon or knife.

Put the fruits in a saucepan with the wine, the remaining bay leaves and the orange rind. Cover and simmer for 5–10 minutes, depending on the firmness of the pears. Leave to cool.

Take the bay leaves out of the cream and discard them. Whip the cream until softly peaking then fold in the orange juice, honey and 3 tablespoons of the cooled wine from the fruit. Chill until needed.

Arrange the fruit in a glass dish and serve with spoonfuls of the bay cream.

WINTER

ROOT VEGETABLES

CARROTS PARSNIPS POTATOES MARROW ONIONS LEEKS SPINACH ARTICHOKES JERUSALEM ARTICHOKES CABBAGE BRUSSELS SPROUTS CELERIAC CELERY

FARE

IN
WINTER

One of the nicest things about winter is the food: comforting dishes make chilly, dull days seem so much better. The delicious flavours of slow-cooked stews and casseroles, hearty pies, soups and crumbles with custard make cold winter days so much more bearable. Winter sees the welcome return of leeks, Brussels sprouts and the first signs of the root vegetables, encouraging us to prepare hearty and nourishing food. As you harvest and start to create space in your allotment, dig the soil over and add well-rotted manure in preparation for the next wave of planting. Remember to harvest red and white cabbages before the hard frosts come and stock up the freezer ready for the Christmas period, so that you can relax and enjoy eating with family and friends.

MAKE THE MOST OF ...

BRUSSELS SPROUTS

Wait until after the first frosts to pick sprouts, so that they are sweet and full of flavour. Work from the bottom upwards and use a sharp knife to remove the firmest sprouts that are about 1 cm/½ inch across. Also remove any dead leaves. Leave sprouts on the plant until they are needed, because they don't store well.

CABBAGES

Most winter cabbages will survive a whole winter outdoors, so they don't need to be stored and can be harvested when needed. Red and white cabbages are the exception, because they need to be cut before the first frost. Cut the cabbage close to the ground using a sharp knife. Store cut cabbages in boxes of straw in a cool, dry place.

CARROTS

Pull carrots up by hand 3–4 months after they have been sown or when they reach the required size. Harvest carrots as you need them, because they keep well in the soil, or you can remove any foliage and store them in boxes in a cool, dry place.

CELERIAC

Celeriac should be harvested when the bulb reaches the same size as a swede or a small football. If your soil is well-drained you can leave celeriac in the ground over winter, but if the ground gets waterlogged it is better to lift them. Use a fork to lift them carefully from the ground, trim off foliage and roots immediately so that the bulb retains the nutrients, and store them in a dry, frost-free place.

JERUSALEM ARTICHOKES

Harvest Jerusalem artichokes when they are needed. They store just as well in the ground, and their flavour is said to be even better after a frost. Harvest them a plant at a time – you should get 10–12 tubers from each plant. They can also be stored in a plastic bag in the refrigerator for a couple of weeks.

LEEKS

Baby leeks can be pulled up easily in the summer, but more mature leeks are ready for pulling in the winter. Wait until they are thick enough for you, and then pull them up by hand. Leeks can be stored whole in the refrigerator for up to 2 weeks. Trim the roots and shoots and wash them thoroughly to remove the dirt before using.

ONIONS

Once the leaves have yellowed and died back onions can be harvested. Lift them from the soil with a fork and spread them out on a path or some spare ground to dry. They can be stored in a cool, dry area, preferably suspended in a net so that air can circulate around them.

PARSNIPS

Leave parsnips in the ground until you want to use them. They are extremely hardy and will survive even the harshest of frosts. If you decide to lift them you can harvest after the first frosts when the roots start to sweeten and the foliage has died back. Use a fork to loosen the soil, remove the foliage and store the roots in boxes in a dry place, making sure that the parsnips aren't touching each other.

POTATOES

The best time to harvest potatoes is several weeks after the plants have died back. Choose a dry day and carefully lift them with a garden fork, taking care not to spear or damage any of the tubers. Check them carefully, discarding any that are diseased, damaged or green. Allow the potatoes to dry for couple of hours before storing them in potato sacks in a cool, dry place until you need them. They should keep for several months.

SWEDES

Harvest your swedes when they are the size of a small melon. Lift them from the soil, using a fork to help you if they are large. Cut off any foliage, which will take nutrients from the vegetable. As with carrots, it is best to store them in the ground until they are needed, because they will just continue to grow and if anything will taste even better.

PAN-FRIED ROOTS WITH CARDAMOM & HONEY

TAKES 25 MINS
SERVES 4

275 g/9 oz carrots, cut into wedges

1 small sweet potato, scrubbed and cut into chunks

275 g/9 oz parsnips, cut into wedges

8 shallots, peeled but left whole

1 tablespoon cardamom pods

2 tablespoons clear honey

2 teaspoons lemon juice

4 tablespoons olive oil

salt and pepper

Cook the carrots, sweet potato, parsnips and shallots in lightly salted boiling water for 7–8 minutes until they are softened but not tender.

Meanwhile, using a pestle and mortar, crush the cardamom pods to release the seeds. Alternatively, crush the pods in a small bowl using the end of a rolling pin. Pick out and discard the pods, then pound the seeds to crush them slightly. Mix the crushed seeds with the honey, lemon juice and a little salt and pepper.

Drain the vegetables. Heat the oil in a large frying pan. Add the vegetables and fry for about 6 minutes until golden, stirring frequently. Add the cardamom dressing and toss together for 1 minute. Serve hot.

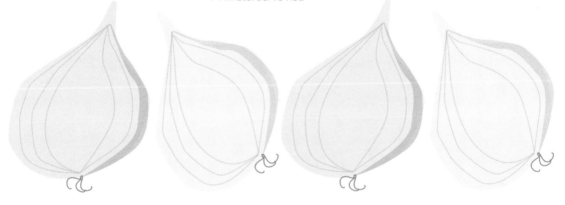

TAKES 1–1¼ HRS
SERVES 4

1 kg/2 lb mixed winter
vegetables, such as carrots,
parsnips, swede and turnips

12 new potatoes, halved if large

2 small onions, cut into wedges

12 garlic cloves, unpeeled

sprigs of thyme and rosemary

3 bay leaves

olive oil, to drizzle

salt and pepper

SOURED CREAM AND CHIVE SAUCE

300 ml/½ pint soured cream

bunch of chives, snipped

Trim the vegetables and cut them into pieces, keeping them roughly the same size as the potatoes so they will cook evenly. Place the winter vegetables, potatoes, onions, garlic, herbs, oil and salt and pepper in a large roasting tin and toss until well coated with oil.

Roast the vegetables in a preheated oven, 230°C/450°F/Gas Mark 8, for 50–60 minutes, stirring from time to time, until all the vegetables are tender.

Meanwhile, make the sauce. Mix together the soured cream and chives and season with salt and pepper. Cover and chill until needed. Serve the vegetables with the sauce for dipping.

ROASTED WINTER VEGETABLES WITH SOURED CREAM & CHIVE SAUCE

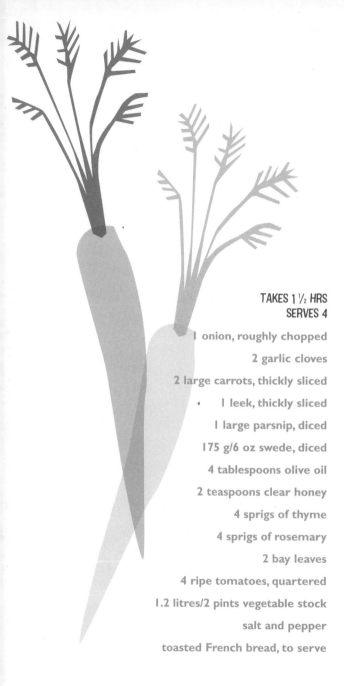

Toss the vegetables with the oil and honey and put them in a roasting tin. Add the thyme, rosemary and bay leaves and cook in a preheated oven, 200°C/ 400°F/Gas Mark 6, for 25–30 minutes. Add the tomatoes and roast for a further 25–30 minutes until all the vegetables are golden and tender. Reduce the oven temperature to 190°C/375°F/ Gas Mark 5.

Discard the herbs and put the vegetables into a food processor or blender. Add half the stock and whizz until smooth, then blend in the remaining stock.

Transfer the soup to a casserole, season to taste with salt and pepper and bake for 20 minutes or until heated through. Serve with toasted French bread.

OVEN-BAKED SOUP

TAKES 1 ½ HRS
SERVES 4

I onion, roughly chopped

2 garlic cloves

2 large carrots, thickly sliced

I leek, thickly sliced

I large parsnip, diced

175 g/6 oz swede, diced

4 tablespoons olive oil

2 teaspoons clear honey

4 sprigs of thyme

4 sprigs of rosemary

2 bay leaves

4 ripe tomatoes, quartered

1.2 litres/2 pints vegetable stock

salt and pepper

toasted French bread, to serve

CURRIED WINTER VEGETABLE SOUP

TAKES 45–50 MINS
SERVES 4

40 g/1 ½ oz ghee or butter

1 onion, chopped

2 garlic cloves, crushed

2 teaspoons grated fresh root ginger

1 large potato, diced

1 large carrot, diced

2 teaspoons ground coriander

1 teaspoon ground cumin

½ teaspoon garam masala

125 g/4 oz red lentils

600 ml/1 pint vegetable stock

600 ml/1 pint tomato juice

salt and pepper

TO SERVE

raita

naan bread

Melt the ghee or butter in a large saucepan and fry the onion, garlic, ginger, potato and carrot for 10 minutes. Stir in the spices and then add the lentils, stock and tomato juice. Bring to the boil, cover and simmer over a low heat for 20–25 minutes until the lentils and vegetables are cooked.

Season to taste with salt and pepper, then spoon into warm bowls. Top each bowl with some raita and serve with naan bread.

CARROTS

CARROTS ARE OFFICIALLY THE WORLD'S FAVOURITE
VEGETABLE. THEY ARE EASY TO GROW AND TASTE
DELICIOUS, ESPECIALLY WHEN THEY ARE FRESHLY
HARVESTED. THEY ARE ALSO EXTREMELY VERSATILE IN
THE KITCHEN, SO WHETHER YOU FANCY MAKING A CAKE,
A ROAST DINNER OR SIMPLY A JUICE, YOU CAN'T GO
WRONG WITH CARROTS. THIS IS PROBABLY JUST AS
WELL, BECAUSE MOST PEOPLE WHO GROW CARROTS
USUALLY FIND THEY HAVE A GLUT TO HARVEST AND FIND
USES FOR.
THE ANCESTOR OF THE CARROT, THE WILD CARROT,
ORIGINATED IN AFGHANISTAN. THEY WERE ORIGINALLY
GROWN FOR THEIR SEEDS AND LEAVES, RATHER THAN
THE ORANGE ROOT THAT WE USE SO MUCH TODAY. THE
MODERN CARROT WAS DOCUMENTED IN EUROPE
SOMEWHERE AROUND THE 9TH CENTURY, BUT IT
WASN'T UNTIL THE 15TH OR 16TH CENTURY THAT THE
CARROT BECAME A POPULAR FOOD.

GOOD FOR YOU

Carrots are rich in beta-carotene, which the body metabolizes into vitamin A. Lack of vitamin A can lead to poor eyesight, hence the belief that eating large amounts of carrots will enable you to see in the dark. They also contain vitamins B and C. Carrots are full of antioxidants and minerals that help combat serious diseases, and they contain dietary fibre that can help with digestive problems. Carrots are more nutritious eaten raw than cooked.

FIVE OF THE BEST

Thumbelina This small, round, sweet carrot is ideal for growing in shallow containers.

Long Red Surrey A delicious, flavoursome cultivar with a yellow core.

Autumn King A heavy yielding, maincrop carrot with long, tapered roots. They can be left in the ground over winter.

Adelaide This early cultivar has a smooth skin and a sweet flavour.

Flyaway A sweet carrot with blunt ends and a good colour. This cultivar has good resistance to carrot fly.

DELICIOUS IDEAS TO TRY

Crisps Use a mandolin to cut some carrots and sweet potatoes into fine slices. Dab them dry on kitchen paper, then sprinkle with chilli powder and olive oil and roast in a hot oven for about 20 minutes until golden.

Salad Grate some carrots and add raisins and mayonnaise for a delicious accompaniment to quiche, cold meat or fish.

Roast Sprinkle your carrots with some cumin seeds and a dash of oil and roast in a moderate oven until tender and sweet.

Juice Wash and trim your carrots and juice them. Carrot juice is delicious combined with freshly squeezed orange or apple juice (see page 12).

Steam One of the best ways to cook carrots is to steam them. Try steaming chopped carrots with some fresh herbs and lemon for a fragrant and tasty accompaniment.

TOP TIPS FOR CARROTS

Use carrot juice to sweeten flapjacks, cakes, sauces and stuffings.

Remove the greenery from carrots as soon as possible after harvesting because it will take all the nutrients and minerals from the orange root.

Store carrots away from other vegetables and fruit because the gases they give off can make the carrots bitter.

Blanch carrots before freezing.

TAKES 45 MINS
SERVES 4

2 tablespoons olive oil

1 large onion, chopped

1–2 garlic cloves, crushed

1 tablespoon finely grated
fresh root ginger

375 g/12 oz carrots, sliced

900 ml/1 ½ pints vegetable
stock

2 tablespoons lime juice or
lemon juice

salt and pepper

TO SERVE

soured cream

2 spring onions, finely
chopped

CARROT & GINGER SOUP

Heat the oil in a large, heavy-based saucepan, add the onion, garlic and ginger and cook over a moderate heat for 5 minutes or until the onions have softened.

Add the carrots and stock and bring to the boil. Reduce the heat and simmer for 15–20 minutes or until the carrots are tender.

Put the soup in a food processor or blender and whizz with the lime or lemon juice, in batches if necessary, until smooth. Strain through a sieve into the pan.

Reheat the soup gently, then serve it in warm bowls with a spoonful of soured cream and sprinkled with finely chopped spring onions.

SNAPPER WITH CARROTS & CARAWAY

TAKES 20 MINS
SERVES 4

500 g/1 lb carrots, sliced

2 teaspoons caraway seeds

4 red snapper fillets, each about 175 g/6 oz

2 oranges

bunch of coriander, roughly chopped, plus extra to garnish

4 tablespoons olive oil

salt and pepper

🌿 Heat a ridged griddle pan over a medium heat. Add the sliced carrots and cook for 3 minutes on each side, adding the caraway seeds for the last 2 minutes of cooking. Transfer to a bowl and keep warm.

🌿 Add the fish fillets to the pan and cook for 3 minutes on each side.

🌿 Meanwhile, squeeze the juice from 1 of the oranges into a bowl. Cut the other orange into quarters. Add the orange quarters to the pan for the last 2 minutes of cooking and cook until charred.

🌿 Add the coriander to the carrots and mix well. Season to taste with salt and pepper and stir in the oil and orange juice. Serve the snapper with the carrots and griddled orange quarters, garnished with chopped coriander.

MINI CARROT & PARSNIP PIES

TAKES 2 HRS
SERVES 6

375 g/12 oz shortcrust pastry, thawed if frozen

375 g/12 oz puff pastry, thawed if frozen

1 egg, lightly beaten

FILLING

4 tablespoons olive oil

500 g/1 lb button mushrooms, quartered

1 onion, finely chopped

2 garlic cloves, crushed

1 tablespoon chopped thyme

250 g/8 oz carrots, chopped

250 g/8 oz parsnips, chopped

150 ml/¼ pint red wine

500 ml/17 fl oz passata (puréed tomatoes)

salt and pepper

Prepare the filling. Heat half the oil in a flameproof casserole and fry the mushrooms with a little salt and pepper for 4–5 minutes until golden. Remove with a slotted spoon and set aside. Add the remaining oil to the pan and fry the onion, garlic and thyme for 5 minutes. Add the carrots and parsnips to the pan and fry for a further 5 minutes until softened and lightly golden.

Pour the wine into the pan and boil rapidly for 3 minutes, then stir in the passata, mushrooms and more salt and pepper. Bring to the boil, cover and simmer for 20 minutes. Remove the lid and cook for a further 20 minutes or until the vegetables are tender and the sauce is really thick. Set aside to cool completely.

Cut the shortcrust pastry into 6 equal pieces and roll them out on a lightly floured surface. Use the pastry to line 6 individual pie dishes, each 12 cm /5 inches across. Divide the puff pastry into 6 and roll each piece out thinly so that each piece is slightly larger than the dishes.

Fill the pies with the cooled vegetable stew. Brush around the rim of the pastry with beaten egg and top with the puff pastry, pressing the edges together to seal. Trim off the excess pastry with a sharp knife and cut a small slit in the centre of each pie. Brush the tops with the beaten egg and bake in a preheated oven, 220°C/425°F/Gas Mark 7, for 25 minutes until golden. Serve hot.

TAKES 40 MINS
SERVES 4

25 g/1 oz butter

**50 g/2 oz fresh root ginger,
peeled and thinly sliced**

bunch of spring onions

500 g/1 lb parsnips, sliced

1 litre/1³/₄ pints vegetable stock

salt and pepper

crème fraîche, to serve

Melt the butter in a large, heavy-based saucepan. Add the ginger and cook over a moderate heat, stirring, for 1 minute. Reserve 1 spring onion, roughly chop the remainder and add to the pan with the parsnips. Cook, stirring, for 2 minutes.

Add the stock and bring to the boil, then reduce the heat, cover and simmer gently for 15 minutes or until the parsnips are tender.

Meanwhile, shred the reserved spring onion lengthways into fine ribbons.

Put the soup in a food processor or blender and whizz, in batches if necessary, until smooth, then return it to the pan. Season to taste with salt and pepper and reheat gently for 1 minute.

Ladle the soup into warm bowls and serve topped with a spoonful of crème fraîche and scattered with spring onion ribbons.

PARSNIP
& GINGER
SOUP

Cut the parsnips into pieces about 5 x 1 cm/2 inches x ½ inch. Put them into a pan of boiling water and parboil for 4 minutes. Drain well and leave to dry.

Transfer the parsnips to a roasting tin large enough to hold them in a single layer. Spoon over the olive oil and sprinkle with the thyme. Toss to coat. Place the parsnips in a preheated oven, 200°C/ 400°F/ Gas Mark 6, and roast for 45–60 minutes, stirring occasionally, until they are tender and lightly patched with brown. Transfer the cooked parsnips to a bowl and leave to cool slightly.

Add the lemon rind and juice and the garlic to the parsnips and season with coarse sea salt and pepper. Toss well and leave to cool.

Serve the dressed parsnips either as they are, or arrange them on a bed of rocket or other salad leaves. If liked, sprinkle wafer-thin shavings of Parmesan over the parsnips before serving them.

TAKES 1–1¼ HRS, PLUS COOLING
SERVES 4–6

750 g/1½ lb parsnips

6 tablespoons olive oil

1 tablespoon roughly chopped thyme

1 teaspoon finely grated lemon rind

2 tablespoons lemon juice

1 garlic clove, crushed

coarse sea salt and pepper

TO GARNISH

rocket or other salad leaves (optional)

50 g/2 oz Parmesan cheese (optional)

ROAST PARSNIPS DRESSED WITH LEMON & GARLIC

CURRIED PARSNIP & CHEESE SOUFFLÉS

TAKES 1¼ HR
SERVES 6

250 g/8 oz peeled parsnips, chopped

25 g/1 oz butter, plus extra for greasing

25 g/1 oz plain flour

2 teaspoons hot curry paste

200 ml/7 fl oz milk

40 g/1½ oz Gruyére or Cheddar cheese, grated

3 eggs, separated

2 tablespoons chopped coriander leaves

40 g/1½ oz ground toasted almonds

salt and pepper

Steam the parsnips for 15–20 minutes until tender. Mash well and set aside to cool.

Melt the butter in a small saucepan. Add the flour and cook for 1 minute. Stir in the curry paste and gradually add the milk, stirring constantly, until smooth. Bring the mixture to the boil, stirring until thickened then cook over a gentle heat for 2 minutes.

Remove the pan from the heat, add the Gruyére or Cheddar and stir until melted. Allow to cool slightly, then beat in the egg yolks with the mashed parsnip, coriander, half the ground almonds and salt and pepper.

Whisk the egg whites until stiff and carefully fold them into the parsnip mixture until evenly incorporated.

Grease 6 large ramekin dishes and line with the remaining ground almonds. Spoon in the soufflé mixture and place the dishes in a large roasting pan. Add enough boiling water to come two-thirds of the way up the sides of the dishes and cook in a preheated oven, 200°C/400°F/Gas Mark 6, for 25 minutes until risen and golden. Serve immediately.

Season the pork steaks with plenty of pepper. Heat the oil in a nonstick frying pan, add the pork steaks and cook for 2 minutes on each side until browned, then transfer to an ovenproof dish.

Mix together the cheese, sage, breadcrumbs and egg yolk in a bowl. Divide the mixture into 4 heaps and use it to top each of the pork steaks, pressing down gently. Cook in a preheated oven, 200°C/ 400°F/Gas Mark 6, for 12–15 minutes until the topping is golden.

Meanwhile, bring a large saucepan of water to the boil, add the parsnips and garlic and cook for 10–12 minutes until tender. Drain and mash with the crème fraîche and plenty of pepper, then serve with the pork steaks and some steamed green beans or cabbage.

TAKES 30 MINS
SERVES 4

4 lean pork steaks, each about 125 g/4 oz

1 teaspoon olive oil

50 g/2 oz crumbly cheese, such as Wensleydale or Cheshire, crumbled

$^1/_2$ tablespoon chopped sage

75 g/3 oz fresh granary breadcrumbs

1 egg yolk, beaten

steamed green beans or cabbage, to serve

PARSNIP PURÉE

625 g/1$^1/_4$ lb parsnips, chopped

2 garlic cloves

3 tablespoons crème fraîche

pepper

CHEESY PORK WITH PARSNIP PURÉE

GOOD

INDIAN SAUTÉED POTATOES

TAKES 30 MINS
SERVES 4

2 tablespoons vegetable oil

I tablespoon finely sliced fresh root ginger

I tablespoon cumin seeds

500 g/I lb potatoes, peeled, cut into 2.5 cm/
I inch cubes and boiled

I fresh green chilli, finely sliced

2 teaspoons lime juice

sea salt and pepper

coriander leaves, to garnish

Heat the oil in a large frying pan. Add the ginger and cumin and stir-fry for 2 minutes.

Add the potatoes and chilli, season to taste with salt and pepper and cook for 6–8 minutes or until the potatoes are lightly browned.

Stir in the lime juice and sprinkle over the coriander leaves. Serve hot.

EATING

Cut the potatoes into 1 cm/½ inch slices, then cut each slice into chunky chips.

Brush a large roasting tin with a little of the oil and heat it in a preheated oven, 220°C/425°F/Gas Mark 7, for 5 minutes.

Scatter the chips in the tin, drizzle with the remaining oil and sprinkle with the paprika and celery salt. Mix until well coated. Bake the chips for 45 minutes, turning them occasionally, until they are golden. Serve sprinkled with salt and pepper.

OVEN-BAKED CHUNKY POTATO CHIPS

TAKES 1 HR
SERVES 4

1 kg/2 lb baking potatoes

150 ml/½ pint mild olive oil or groundnut oil

1 teaspoon ground paprika

1 teaspoon celery salt

salt and pepper

FISH PIE

TAKES 1³/₄ HRS, PLUS INFUSING
SERVES 6

1 kg/2 lb cod fillet, skinned

3 tablespoons milk

275 g/9 oz scallops or raw
peeled prawns

1.25 kg/2¹/₂ lb floury potatoes

25 g /1 oz butter

3 large shallots, finely chopped

4 tablespoons chopped tarragon

4 tablespoons chopped parsley

125 g/4 oz Gruyére cheese,
grated

salt and pepper

BÉCHAMEL SAUCE

200 ml/7 fl oz milk

2 bay leaves

1 small onion, quartered

1 teaspoon black peppercorns

50 g/2 oz butter

40 g/1¹/₂ oz plain flour

300 ml/¹/₂ pint single cream

grated nutmeg

Make the béchamel sauce. Put the milk in a saucepan with the bay leaves, onion and peppercorns. Bring it almost to the boil, then remove the pan from the heat and leave to infuse for 15 minutes. Strain through a sieve.

Melt the butter in a heavy-based saucepan. Tip in the flour and stir it in quickly. Cook gently for 1 minute. Remove the pan from the heat and stir in the strained milk, then the cream. Return the pan to the heat and cook gently, stirring continuously, until thickened and smooth. Season to taste with nutmeg and salt and pepper. Cover and keep warm.

Put the cod in a frying pan with the milk and season with salt and pepper. Cover the pan and cook gently for 5 minutes. Add the scallops or prawns and cook, covered, for a further 2 minutes. Remove the cod and scallops or prawns and leave to cool, reserving the liquid.

Bring a saucepan of lightly salted water to the boil. Thinly slice the potatoes and add them to the pan. Return to the boil and cook the potatoes for 6–8 minutes or until just tender. Drain. Melt the butter in the rinsed-out frying pan and fry the shallots for 5 minutes. Stir in the tarragon and parsley.

Flake the fish into large chunks, discarding any bones, and arrange in a large, shallow, ovenproof dish. Add the scallops or prawns, shallots and herbs.

Stir two-thirds of the Gruyére into the béchamel sauce along with the poaching juices. Pour half over the fish. Layer the potatoes over the top and pour over the remaining sauce. Scatter with the rest of the cheese and bake the pie in a preheated oven, 190°C/375°F/Gas Mark 5, for about 40 minutes or until golden.

TAKES 2¼ HRS, PLUS STANDING
MAKES ABOUT 2.75 KG/6 LB

1 marrow, about 2 kg/4 lb, peeled, halved
lengthways and seeded

1 kg/2 lb small pickling onions, halved

1 green or red pepper, cored, deseeded and
finely chopped

250 g/8 oz pitted dates, finely chopped

1 tablespoon freshly grated root ginger

600 ml/1 pint white wine vinegar

500 g/1 lb demerara sugar

salt

🌿 Cut the marrow flesh into chunks and layer with the onions in a large bowl, salting each layer, then cover the bowl and leave overnight. The next day, lightly rinse and thoroughly dry the vegetables.

🌿 Put the salted vegetables into a large pan. Add the pepper and dates to the pan with the ginger, vinegar and sugar. Bring the mixture to the boil, stirring well to mix the ingredients. Reduce the heat, cover the pan and simmer, stirring frequently, for 1½ hours, until the mixture has thickened.

🌿 Transfer the pickle to warm, dry jars and top with airtight lids. Label and leave to mature in a cool, dark place for 2 weeks before using or store, unopened, for about 6 months.

MARROW & ONION PICKLE

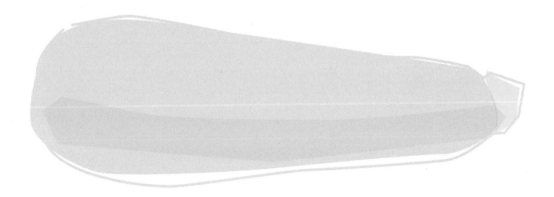

RED ONIONS STUFFED WITH MUSHROOMS & RED RICE

TAKES 2 HRS
SERVES 4

4 large red onions, peeled and left whole

2 tablespoons olive oil

125 g/4 oz mushrooms, finely chopped

75 g/3 oz red or brown rice

1 tablespoon chopped parsley

300 ml/½ pint water

1 tablespoon seedless sultanas (optional)

1 tablespoon grated Parmesan cheese

salt and pepper

TO SERVE

olive oil

coriander leaves

Cut the top off each onion and scoop out the centre with a teaspoon. Finely chop the scooped-out onion. Heat the oil in a large frying pan and gently fry the chopped onion until soft and golden brown. Add the mushrooms and cook for 5 minutes, stirring frequently, until they are done.

Meanwhile, put the onion cups into a saucepan of boiling water and simmer for 10 minutes or until they begin to soften. Drain well.

Add the rice, parsley and measured water to the mushrooms with salt and pepper to taste. Bring to the boil and boil for 5 minutes, then cover the pan and simmer for 30 minutes or until the rice is soft. Add more water if the rice looks dry.

Stir the sultanas (if used) into the rice mixture then spoon the mixture into the onion cups.

Put the stuffed onions into a roasting tin, cover with foil and bake in a preheated oven, 190°C/375°F/Gas Mark 5, for 30 minutes. Remove the foil, sprinkle the onions with grated Parmesan and cook for 10 minutes. Serve the onions drizzled with extra oil and garnished with coriander.

TAKES 45–50 MINS
SERVES 2

2 x 25 cm/10 inch ready-made pizza bases

125 g/4 oz baby rocket leaves

1 tablespoon extra olive oil

squeeze of lemon juice

15 g/½ oz shaved Parmesan cheese

TOPPING

4 tablespoons olive oil, plus extra to drizzle

4 onions, thinly sliced

6 garlic cloves, halved or quartered

1 tablespoon chopped sage

50 g/2 oz semi-dried tomatoes

75 g/3 oz pitted black olives

¼ teaspoon dried chilli flakes

salt and pepper

🌿 Prepare the topping. Heat the oil in a frying pan and fry the onions, garlic, sage with salt and pepper to taste over a medium heat for 25 minutes until golden and caramelized. Set aside to cool.

🌿 Top each pizza base with half the onion mixture and half the tomatoes, olives and chilli flakes. Drizzle over a little extra oil.

🌿 Carefully slide a pizza base on to a preheated pizza stone or baking sheet and bake on the middle shelf of a preheated oven, 200°C/400°F/Gas Mark 6, for 10–12 minutes until the dough is cooked. Repeat to cook a second pizza.

🌿 Meanwhile, toss the rocket with the oil, lemon juice, salt and pepper and some shaved Parmesan. Serve the pizzas topped with the rocket salad.

CARAMELIZED ONION PIZZA

WHITE ONION SOUP

TAKES 1½ HRS
SERVES 4–6

50 g/2 oz butter

500 g/1 lb onions, finely sliced

1 leek, white part only,
about 50 g/2 oz in total,
thinly sliced

40 g/1½ oz plain flour

1 litre/1¾ pints chicken stock

150 ml/¼ pint single cream,
plus extra to garnish

salt and white pepper

croûtons, to serve

🌿 Melt the butter in a large, heavy-based pan. Add the onions and leek. Cover tightly and cook over a low heat, stirring frequently, for about 30 minutes. Do not allow the onions and leek to brown.

🌿 Sprinkle the flour over the onions and leek and stir well to mix. Gradually add the stock. Bring the stock to the boil, then reduce the heat and simmer for 15 minutes.

🌿 Season the soup with salt and pepper to taste, add the cream and reheat without boiling. Serve the soup garnished with a swirl of cream and scattered with croûtons.

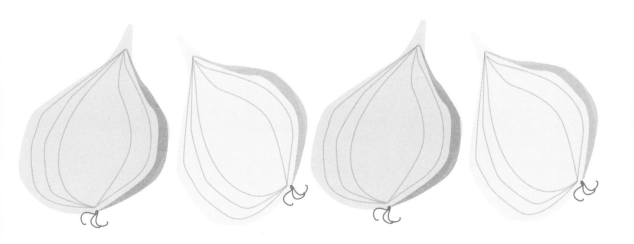

Heat the oil in a saucepan, add the leeks and peppers and stir well. Cover and cook very gently for 10 minutes.

Add the vinegar to the pan and cook, uncovered, for a further 10 minutes. The vegetables should be brown from the vinegar and all the liquid should have evaporated.

Season well with salt and pepper, then stir in the parsley and serve immediately.

TAKES 25 MINS
SERVES 4

2 tablespoons olive oil

2 leeks, cut into 1 cm/¹/₂ inch pieces

1 orange pepper, cored, deseeded and cut into 1 cm/¹/₂ inch chunks

1 red pepper, cored, deseeded and cut into 1 cm/¹/₂ inch chunks

3 tablespoons balsamic vinegar

handful of flat leaf parsley, chopped

salt and pepper

BALSAMIC BRAISED LEEKS & PEPPERS

CHESHIRE CHEESE & LEEK TART

TAKES 1½ HRS
SERVES 6

PASTRY

125 g/4 oz self-raising flour

50 g /2 oz oatmeal

75 g/3 oz chilled butter, diced

FILLING

3 tablespoons olive oil

2 garlic cloves, chopped

3 leeks, trimmed, cleaned and sliced

2 teaspoons chopped rosemary

2 eggs, beaten

150 ml/¼ pint milk

125 g/4 oz Cheshire cheese, crumbled

2 tablespoons grated Parmesan cheese

salt and pepper

Mix the flour and oatmeal in a bowl. Add the butter and rub it in with your fingertips until the mixture resembles breadcrumbs. Add enough cold water, about 2–3 tablespoons, to mix to a firm dough. Turn the dough out on to a lightly floured surface and knead briefly.

Roll out the pastry and line a 23 cm/9 inch pie dish. Make cuts around the pastry rim at 2.5 cm/1 inch intervals, brush the rim with water, then fold every other piece of pastry upwards and seal. Fill the pastry case with crumpled foil and bake in a preheated oven 200°C/400°F/Gas Mark 6, for 15 minutes, then remove the foil and return the pastry case to the oven for 5 minutes. Set the pastry case aside. Reduce the oven temperature to 180°C/350°F/Gas Mark 4.

Make the filling. Heat the oil in a frying pan over a moderate heat and soften the garlic. Add the leeks and cook gently for 7–10 minutes until softened. Stir in the rosemary and season to taste with salt and pepper, then spread the filling over the tart case.

Beat the eggs, milk and Cheshire cheese in a bowl then pour the mixture into the pastry case over the filling. Sprinkle with Parmesan cheese and bake for 30–35 minutes, until the filling is set and golden brown. Serve the tart warm or cold.

LAMB & LEEK STEW WITH ROSEMARY DUMPLINGS

TAKES 2½ HRS, PLUS CHILLING
SERVES 4

875 g/1¾ lb breast of lamb

2 tablespoons vegetable oil

1 onion, chopped

400 g/13 oz carrots, sliced

2 celery sticks, sliced

3 bay leaves

1.5 litres/2½ pints water

75 g/3 oz pearl barley

425 g/14 oz small leeks, sliced

salt and pepper

DUMPLINGS

150 g/5 oz self-raising flour

75 g/3 oz beef or vegetable suet

2 teaspoons chopped rosemary

125 ml/4 fl oz water

Cut the lamb into chunks. Heat 1 tablespoon oil in a large, heavy-based frying pan and fry the lamb until it is well browned. Using a slotted spoon, remove the lamb chunks and transfer to a large saucepan.

Drain the excess fat from the pan and fry the onion for 5 minutes. Add the carrots, celery, bay leaves and measured water, bring to the boil then pour over the lamb. Stir in the pearl barley and a little salt and pepper and bring to a gentle simmer. Cover with a lid and cook on the lowest possible heat for about 1 hour until the lamb is tender.

Meanwhile, fry the leeks in the remaining oil and add them to the stew. Cook the stew for a further 15 minutes, leave to cool, then tip into a bowl and chill overnight.

Make the dumplings. Mix together the flour, suet and rosemary with a little salt and add the water to make a firm paste. Remove the layer of fat from the stew, return the stew to the pan and bring it slowly to a simmer.

Use a dessertspoon to place 8 scoops of the dumpling paste over the stew. Cover and simmer gently until the dumplings are light and fluffy. Serve the stew in shallow bowls.

LAMB NOISETTES WITH LEEKS & CAPERS

TAKES 30 MINS
SERVES 4

8 loin lamb chops

3 tablespoons redcurrant jelly

1 tablespoon olive oil

25 g/1 oz butter

2 leeks, thinly sliced

1 tablespoon capers, drained and rinsed

small handful of rosemary or mint leaves, plus extra to garnish

2 teaspoons pink peppercorns in brine, drained

salt and pepper

Roll up the lamb chops tightly and secure them with 2 cocktail sticks. Put the noisettes on a foil-lined grill pan, dot with the redcurrant jelly and season to taste with salt and pepper. Cook under a preheated hot grill for 5 minutes then turn them over, spoon the redcurrant jelly juices over the lamb and cook for 5 minutes more.

Meanwhile, heat the oil and butter in a frying pan. Add the leeks, capers, snipped herbs and peppercorns and stir-fry for 5 minutes until the leeks have softened and are just beginning to brown. Spoon on to individual plates.

Arrange the lamb noisettes on top of the leeks, remove the cocktail sticks and sprinkle with extra snipped herbs.

Lightly coat the liver in the seasoned flour. Heat half the oil in a nonstick frying pan, add the liver and cook for 3–4 minutes on each side or until cooked to your liking. Remove from the pan to a warm plate and keep warm in a low oven.

Heat the remaining oil in the frying pan, add the leeks and bacon and cook for 3–4 minutes.

Stir in the beans and crème fraîche, season to taste with pepper and heat through. Serve with the liver, garnished with the parsley or thyme and accompanied by a green salad.

TAKES 30 MINS
SERVES 2

about 250 g/8 oz calves' liver

2 tablespoons seasoned flour

2 teaspoons olive oil

8 baby leeks or 2 large leeks, sliced

2 rashers of lean back bacon, chopped

250 g/8 oz can cannellini beans, drained and rinsed

2 tablespoons crème fraîche

pepper

2 tablespoons chopped parsley or thyme, to garnish

green salad, to serve

CALVES' LIVER WITH LEEKS & BEANS

DIG FOR YO

VICHYSSOISE

TAKES 1 HR, PLUS CHILLING
SERVES 6

1 kg/2 lb leeks

50 g/2 oz butter

1 onion, chopped

1 litre/1³/₄ pints vegetable stock

pinch of grated nutmeg

750 g/1¹/₂ lb old potatoes, diced

600 ml/1 pint milk

300 ml/¹/₂ pint single cream

150 ml/¹/₄ pint double cream, chilled

salt and white pepper

2 tablespoons snipped chives, to garnish

Slice off the green tops of the leeks and set them aside for use in another recipe. Thinly slice the white parts of the leeks.

Melt the butter in a large, heavy-based saucepan. Add the leeks and onion and cook over a moderate heat for 5 minutes or until softened but not coloured.

Add the stock, nutmeg and potatoes and season to taste with salt and pepper. Bring to the boil. Reduce the heat, partially cover the pan and simmer for 25 minutes. Pour in the milk and simmer for 5–8 minutes. Leave to cool slightly.

Put the soup in a food processor or blender and whizz, in batches if necessary, until smooth, then rub it through a sieve into a bowl. Add the single cream, stir well and cover closely.

Chill the soup in the refrigerator for at least 3 hours. Just before serving, swirl in the double cream then taste and adjust the seasoning if necessary. Serve the soup in chilled bowls, garnishing each portion with a generous sprinkling of snipped chives.

UR DINNER

4 small Jerusalem artichokes

2 tablespoons walnut oil

8 slices of smoked pancetta

40 g/1 ¹/₂ oz shelled walnuts

4–6 tablespoons olive oil

1 garlic clove, crushed

2 tablespoons balsamic vinegar

125 g/4 oz baby spinach leaves

50 g/2 oz watercress

4 tablespoons chopped mixed herbs, such as basil, mint and parsley

salt and pepper

Scrub the artichokes and cut them into 5 mm/¼ inch thick slices. Toss with the walnut oil in a roasting tin and roast in a preheated oven, 200°C/400°F/Gas Mark 6, for 20 minutes, turning after 10 minutes.

Meanwhile, grill the pancetta until crisp, then break it into bite-sized pieces. Dry-fry the walnuts until evenly browned. Set aside.

Heat 1 tablespoon of the oil in a small pan and fry the garlic for 1 minute, until lightly golden. Add the vinegar and the remaining olive oil, season to taste with salt and pepper and keep warm.

Put the spinach and watercress in a large bowl, add the pancetta, walnuts, artichokes and herbs and mix well. Drizzle with the warm dressing. Serve immediately.

SPINACH, ARTICHOKE & BACON SALAD

JERUSALEM ARTICHOKE SOUP

TAKES 1–1¼ HRS
SERVES 6

I kg/2 lb Jerusalem artichokes

lemon juice

50 g/2 oz butter

I onion, chopped

600 ml/I pint vegetable stock

600 ml/I pint milk

150 ml/¼ pint single cream

salt and white pepper

TO GARNISH

finely chopped parsley

croûtons

If the artichokes are fairly smooth, peel them and drop immediately into acidulated water (with lemon juice) to prevent discoloration. If they are knobbly, scrub them in plenty of water and cut off the dark tips and any small, dry roots. Slice the artichokes and drop immediately into acidulated water.

Melt the butter in a large, heavy-based saucepan. Add the onion and cook over a moderate heat for 5 minutes or until softened. Add the drained artichokes and cook, stirring, for 3 minutes. Season to taste with salt and pepper. Add the stock and milk and bring to simmering point, stirring constantly. Reduce the heat, partially cover and simmer for 30 minutes or until the vegetables are tender.

Put the soup in a food processor or blender and whizz briefly, in batches if necessary, then transfer it to a clean saucepan. Reheat gently without boiling, then add the cream. Serve the soup in warm bowls, garnished with finely chopped parsley and croûtons.

CABBAGES

CABBAGE IS AN UNDERUSED AND UNDERRATED VEGETABLE, WHICH CAN BE ADDED TO DOZENS OF DIFFERENT RECIPES, FROM SOUPS TO SOUFFLÉS. MANY PEOPLE ASSOCIATE EATING CABBAGE WITH THE OVERCOOKED LEAVES THAT WERE PUT ON THEIR SCHOOL DINNER PLATE, BUT COOKED CAREFULLY, CABBAGE IS A DELICIOUS AND NUTRITIOUS ADDITION TO ANY MEAL. BY CAREFUL SOWING IT'S POSSIBLE TO HAVE FRESH CABBAGES AVAILABLE ALMOST ALL YEAR ROUND.

THE CABBAGE IS THOUGHT TO BE RELATED TO A WILD MUSTARD PLANT THAT GREW IN MEDITERRANEAN COUNTRIES, AND IT WAS USED BY THE ANCIENT GREEKS AND THE ROMANS WHO APPRECIATED ITS MEDICINAL AND CULINARY QUALITIES.

GOOD FOR YOU

Cabbages are one of the best sources of vitamins. They contain vitamins A, B, C and E, which have benefits for the skin, eyes and nervous system. Cabbage can boost the immune system, helping it to fight off antibodies, and it is also rich in minerals that cleanse the digestive system. Cabbage leaves placed on the breast can help pregnant women if they have engorgement from breastfeeding. The natural chemicals found in cabbage are also thought to protect against certain types of cancers and other serious diseases.

FIVE OF THE BEST

Kilaxy This cabbage has tender leaves, a good green colour and a delicious flavour.

Red Flare A reliable red cabbage with a good firm head, which can be cut in mid-autumn and throughout winter.

Tundra This frost-hardy cabbage is ready for cutting from late autumn right through to early spring. It has firm, flavoursome leaves.

Ruby Perfection This reliable cabbage with a good flavour is suitable for small plots.

January King This popular drumhead Savoy type of winter cabbage has crisp, reddish leaves.

DELICIOUS IDEAS TO TRY

Sauté Chop up a cabbage, add it to a hot wok with a little oil, sauté until it begins to wilt, then season with ginger, garlic and lemon juice to taste.

Coleslaw Shred half a cabbage, an onion and 2 large carrots. Add mayonnaise, white wine vinegar and salt and pepper to taste.

Braised Chop half a head of red cabbage and place in a large pan with some butter, a dash of water, a dash of balsamic vinegar and a peeled and chopped cooking apple. Cook over a high heat for 15–20 minutes.

Bubble and Squeak Mix up leftover cooked potatoes, swede and cabbage. Season to taste and fry with a little butter until golden. Serve with cold meat.

Stir-fry Stir-fry shredded white cabbage, carrot, onion and broccoli with some ginger, garlic and soy sauce. Serve with noodles.

TOP TIPS FOR CABBAGES

Blanch cabbage for only about 3–4 minutes in boiling water. Drain and toss with a little knob of butter.

Red and white cabbages can be cut in winter and stored until early spring in a cool place in crates lined with straw.

Red cabbage is the exception to the rule and should be slow cooked for best results.

CHORIZO, BEAN & CABBAGE SOUP

TAKES 2¼–2¾ HRS, PLUS SOAKING
SERVES 4

**175 g/6 oz dried broad beans, soaked
overnight in cold water**

250 g/8 oz chorizo sausage

2 sprigs of rosemary

1 bouquet garni

1.8 litres/3 pints cold water

**2 tablespoons olive oil, plus extra to
drizzle**

1 onion, chopped

2 garlic cloves, crushed

**1 small red pepper, cored, deseeded
and chopped**

pinch of cayenne pepper

250 g/8 oz, Savoy cabbage, shredded

1 tablespoon chopped parsley

salt and pepper

🌿 Drain and rinse the soaked beans and put them in a saucepan with 125 g/4 oz of the chorizo in one piece, the rosemary, bouquet garni and cold water. Bring to the boil and boil rapidly for 10 minutes, then simmer gently, covered, for 1–1½ hours until the beans are tender.

🌿 Heat the oil in a frying pan and fry the onion, garlic, red pepper and cayenne for 5 minutes. Dice the remaining chorizo, add it to the pan and fry for a further 5 minutes.

🌿 Stir the onion mixture into the cooked beans with the cabbage and season to taste with salt and pepper. Bring to the boil and cook for 20 minutes. Add the parsley, adjust the seasoning to taste and spoon into warm bowls. Drizzle with olive oil and serve immediately with crusty bread.

Drain the soaked beans, rinse and put in a large saucepan. Add the measured water, bring to the boil and boil rapidly for 10 minutes, then reduce the heat to low and simmer gently for 45 minutes.

Meanwhile, toss the onion, garlic and tofu in half the oil and place in a roasting tin. Cook in a preheated oven, 200°C/400°F/Gas Mark 6, for 35 minutes, turning occasionally, until golden.

Heat the remaining oil in a large saucepan. Add the potato and sage and fry for 10 minutes until browned, then stir into the beans with the roasted tofu, cabbage and stock. Season to taste with salt and pepper. Bring to the boil, cover and simmer gently for 20 minutes until the potatoes and cabbage are cooked. Serve hot

CALDO VERDE & SMOKED TOFU SOUP

TAKES 1½ HRS, PLUS SOAKING
SERVES 4–6

125 g/4 oz dried cannellini beans, soaked overnight

1.2 litres/2 pints water

1 small onion, chopped roughly

4 whole garlic cloves

250 g/8 oz smoked tofu (bean curd), diced

2 tablespoons olive oil

1 small potato, diced

1 tablespoon chopped sage

175 g/6 oz Savoy cabbage, shredded roughly

300 ml/½ pint vegetable stock

salt and pepper

500 g/1 lb kale or green leaf cabbage, stalk removed, finely shredded

500 g/1 lb potatoes, unpeeled

6 spring onions or chives, finely chopped

150 ml/¼ pint milk or cream

125 g/4 oz butter

salt and pepper

Cook the kale or cabbage in a large saucepan of lightly salted boiling water for about 10 minutes until very tender. At the same time, cook the potatoes in another pan of lightly salted boiling water until tender.

Put the spring onions or chives and the milk or cream in a pan and simmer over a low heat for about 5 minutes.

Drain the kale or cabbage and mash. Drain the potatoes, peel and mash well. Add the hot milk mixture, beating well to give a soft fluffy texture. Beat in the kale or cabbage, season with salt and pepper and add half the butter. The colcannon should be a speckled, green colour.

Heat the colcannon through thoroughly then serve in individual bowls. Make a well in the centre of each one and add a knob of the remaining butter. Serve immediately.

COLCANNON

RED CABBAGE, APPLE & WENSLEYDALE SALAD

TAKES 17–18 MINS
SERVES 4–6

50 g/2 oz pecan nuts or walnuts, roughly chopped

1 small red cabbage

1 red or white onion, thinly sliced

175 g/6 oz fresh dates, pitted and roughly chopped

1 large red apple, cored, halved and thinly sliced

150 g/5 oz Wensleydale cheese

salt and pepper

DRESSING

3 tablespoons olive oil

2 tablespoons wholegrain mustard

1 tablespoon clear honey

1 teaspoon white wine vinegar or lemon juice

salt and pepper

Put the nuts on a baking sheet and toast under a preheated hot grill for 2–3 minutes until browned. Set aside.

Shred the cabbage as finely as possible and put it in a large salad bowl with the onion, dates and apple. Season with salt and pepper and toss lightly to mix.

Make the dressing. Put all the ingredients in a small bowl and whisk with a balloon whisk or fork until thoroughly blended. Alternatively, put all the ingredients together in a screw-top jar, close the lid tightly and shake until thoroughly combined.

Crumble the Wensleydale over the salad and sprinkle with the reserved nuts. Drizzle with the dressing and serve immediately.

Heat the oil in a large, heavy-based saucepan. Add the bacon and cook over a moderate heat for 5 minutes or until golden. Add the onion and celery, cover and cook, stirring frequently, for 5 minutes. Add the Brussels sprouts and cook for 5–8 minutes.

Stir the measured water into the pan with the potatoes, marjoram and nutmeg and bring to the boil. Reduce the heat and simmer, uncovered, for 30 minutes or until the potatoes are tender. Season to taste with salt and pepper.

Put the soup in a food processor or blender and whizz, in batches if necessary, until smooth, then transfer it to a clean saucepan.

Beat the egg yolk with the milk in a small bowl. Bring the soup to simmering point, then stir in the egg and milk mixture and heat through without boiling. Serve the soup immediately in warm bowls.

TAKES 1 HR
SERVES 6

1 tablespoon olive oil

50 g/2 oz rindless unsmoked streaky bacon, finely chopped

1 onion, chopped

1 celery stick, thinly sliced

375 g/12 oz Brussels sprouts, trimmed and chopped

900 ml/1 ½ pints water

375 g/12 oz potatoes, cut into 1 cm/½ inch cubes

1 teaspoon finely chopped marjoram

pinch of grated nutmeg (or to taste)

1 egg yolk

4 tablespoons milk

salt and white pepper

BRUSSELS SPROUTS & BACON SOUP

Put the Brussels sprouts in a saucepan of lightly salted boiling water. Cover and cook for 10–12 minutes until tender.

Meanwhile, put the chestnuts in a saucepan, add enough vegetable stock to cover and heat gently until warmed through.

Drain the sprouts and the chestnuts. Stir the chestnuts into the sprouts with the butter, season to taste with salt and pepper and serve.

TAKES 20–22 MINS
SERVES 5

750 g/1 ½ lb Brussels sprouts, trimmed

200 g/7 oz can chestnuts, drained

vegetable stock, to cover

15 g/½ oz butter

salt and pepper

BRUSSELS SPROUTS WITH CHESTNUTS

BUTTERY CELERIAC MASH

TAKES 35 MINS
SERVES 4–6

1 kg/2 lb celeriac

500 g/1 lb floury potatoes, cut into chunks

4 tablespoons milk

40 g/1 ¹/₂ oz butter

salt and pepper

Cut away the knobbly skin from the celeriac. Chop the flesh into chunks the same size as the potatoes. Put both vegetables in a saucepan and cover with cold water. Bring to the boil, then reduce the heat and simmer gently for 15–20 minutes or until very tender.

Drain the vegetables well and return them to the pan. Add the milk, butter and a little salt and pepper and mash until very smooth. Reheat gently and serve.

CREAMY CELERIAC DAUPHINOISE WITH NUTMEG & GARLIC

TAKES 55–60 MINS
SERVES 6

1 celeriac, about 625 g/1¼ lb, peeled and thinly sliced

3 spring onions, thinly sliced

250 ml/8 fl oz double cream

3 large garlic cloves, finely chopped

grated nutmeg

25 g/1 oz butter

salt and pepper

Cook the sliced celeriac in a saucepan of boiling water for 3 minutes. Drain in a colander, rinse with cold water and drain again.

Layer the celeriac and spring onions in a lightly buttered ovenproof dish. Mix together the cream, garlic, nutmeg and salt and pepper and pour the mixture over the celeriac. Dot with butter, cover loosely with clingfilm and chill until ready to cook.

Remove the clingfilm and cook the dauphinoise in a preheated oven, 190°C/375°F/Gas Mark 5, for 30–35 minutes until browned on top and the celeriac slices are tender. Serve immediately.

WALNUT PASTRY

150 g/5 oz plain flour

25 g/1 oz walnuts, finely chopped

75 g/3 oz chilled butter, diced

1 teaspoon paprika

FILLING

25 g/1 oz butter

2 shallots, sliced

1 celery stick, finely chopped

125 g/4 oz curd cheese

2 eggs, beaten

150 ml/¼ pint milk

125 g/4 oz Stilton cheese, crumbled

2–3 walnuts, lightly crushed

salt and pepper

Make the pastry. Mix the flour and walnuts in a bowl, add the butter and rub in with your fingertips until the mixture resembles fine breadcrumbs. Stir in the paprika, then add enough cold water, about 2–3 tablespoons, to mix to a firm dough.

Knead the dough briefly on a lightly floured surface, then roll it out and line a 20 cm/8 inch flan tin. Chill for 30 minutes, then fill with crumpled foil and bake in a preheated oven, 200°C/400°F/Gas Mark 6, for 15 minutes. Remove the foil and return the flan case to the oven for 5 minutes. Reduce the oven temperature to 180°C/350°F/Gas Mark 4.

Make the filling. Melt the butter in a saucepan, add the shallots and celery and cook gently for about 5 minutes, until softened. Beat the curd cheese with the eggs in a bowl. Stir in the celery mixture, milk and Stilton and season to taste with salt and pepper.

Pour the filling into the flan case and sprinkle the broken walnuts over the top. Bake for 30 minutes until the filling is firm and golden-brown. Serve warm or cold.

STILTON, CELERY & WALNUT TART

Melt the butter in a saucepan and gently fry the onion, garlic and cumin for 5 minutes until softened. Add the carrot and celery and fry for a further 5 minutes.

Add the lentils to the pan, stir once, then add the stock and bay leaves. Bring the mixture to the boil and simmer for 15 minutes. Stir in the cream, season to taste with salt and pepper and heat through.

Serve the lentils garnished with chopped celery leaves and accompanied by crusty bread.

TAKES 40 MINS
SERVES 4

40 g/1 ½ oz butter

1 onion, finely chopped

1 garlic clove, finely chopped

1 teaspoon ground cumin

1 carrot, diced

2 celery sticks, diced

2 x 400 g/13 oz cans green lentils, rinsed and drained

150 ml/¼ pint vegetable stock

2 bay leaves

125 ml/4 fl oz double cream

salt and pepper

chopped celery leaves, to garnish

crusty bread, to serve

CREAMY LENTILS WITH CELERY

INDEX

ACKNOWLEDGEMENTS

Executive editor Jessica Cowie
Senior editor Lisa John
Deputy Creative Director Karen Sawyer
Designer Miranda Harvey
Production Manager David Hearn
Illustrator Miranda Harvey